THE EXECUTIVE'S
Business Letter Book

Ted Nicholas

Enterprise · Dearborn
a division of Dearborn Publishing Group, Inc.

Published by Enterprise·Dearborn,
a division of Dearborn Publishing Group, Inc.

Printed in the United States of America

92 93 94 10 9 8 7 6 5 4 3 2 1

Library of Congress Cataloging-in-Publication Data

Nicholas, Ted, 1934–
  The executive's business letter book: ready-to-use business
letters for business owners and executives / Ted Nicholas. — [Newly
rev.]
   p. cm.
Includes index.
ISBN 0-79310-491-2 (paper)
1. Commercial correspondence—Handbooks, manuals, etc. I. Title.
HF5726.N53   1992   92-19246
  658.4′53–dc20   CIP

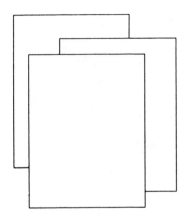

Books by Ted Nicholas

The Complete Book of Corporate Forms

The Complete Guide to Business Agreements

The Complete Guide to Consulting Success (coauthor, Howard Shenson)

The Executive's Business Letter Book

43 Proven Ways To Raise Capital for Your Small Business

The Golden Mailbox: How To Get Rich Direct Marketing Your Product

How To Form Your Own Corporation Without a Lawyer for Under $75.00

How To Get a Top Job in Tough Times (coauthor, Bethany Waller)

How To Get Your Own Trademark

Secrets of Entrepreneurial Leadership: Building Top Performance
Through Trust and Teamwork

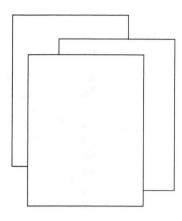

Contents

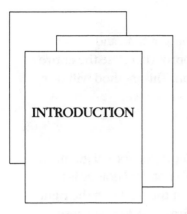

| INTRODUCTION |

Generating Profits with Business Correspondence

Your correspondence is an important business tool. Unfortunately, in many businesses it is an often-ignored business tool.

Everything you do, whether or not it is part of your formal marketing program, sells your business. Letters are no exception. They can be either your most effective salespeople, or they can undo the positive effects of your other promotional efforts. A crisp, clear, concise letter might help convince a banker or supplier to give you credit. But carelessly written correspondence will make the reader feel uneasy about lending money to the writer. A well-written response to a complaint could retain a customer. An ineffective response results in a lost customer plus some negative word-of-mouth advertising.

Letters also provide a complete record of your business transactions. If there is a dispute over what was done or promised, a review of past correspondence can resolve the disagreement. An understandable and complete letter will set both parties straight and, perhaps, keep the dispute out of court. But if you avoid writing letters or do not write good letters, it might be difficult to amicably settle the matter.

This book is designed to help you get the best results from your correspondence. It contains model letters for almost any situation that arises in business. With a model letter to work from, you will be able to write an effective letter for any situation without wasting time, money, or labor.

How to Use This Book

The model letters in this book are taken from actual business letters that have proven their effectiveness under fire in genuine business situations. Using these letters ensures that you have a specific letter available for every situation—whether it is routine or a special case. You are also assured that your letters will be well-written and will convey the right image for your firm. There is no risk that the reader will be annoyed by or receive a bad impression from an imperfect letter.

When a situation calls for a letter, consult the table of contents to locate the

1

appropriate model letter. Read the letter and notice its style, content, and organization. Then you can adapt the letter as you think appropriate. Use the entire letter or choose only paragraphs that apply to your situation. This method will save a great deal of time and ensure that your correspondence is effective.

Some Tips on Letter Writing

The mistake many business writers make is thinking that proper, formal grammar is the most important part of an effective business letter. It's not. Psychology is the most important asset of the business writer. You want to put the reader in the right frame of mind and generate positive attitudes about your firm. Stiff, formal prose won't do that.

Here's how to write business letters that work:

Talk to your reader. Even if you don't know the reader or are writing a form letter, try to picture the reader. The letter is more interesting to write and read when it is written with an individual in mind. More important, a letter will be more compelling when you visualize a reader before writing.

Don't hesitate to write the word "you." Formal prose should be written in the third person, but an effective business letter will talk directly to the reader. After writing a letter, count the number of times "you" appears. Is the letter written directly to the reader? Does the letter make the reader feel involved?

Hit the ground running. The opening paragraph is the most important part of your letter. If the reader is to respond the way you want, the opening sentences must grab his attention and put him in the right mood. You must make the reader want to read the entire letter carefully.

Don't squander this opportunity by starting your letter with standard phrases such as "In regard to your letter of..." And don't use the opening paragraph as a filler. Your first sentence should tell the reader of a valuable benefit you can give him; ask an intriguing question; make a shocking statement; or contain relevant humor. The first paragraph usually requires more time and attention from the writer than does the rest of the letter.

Be positive and enthusiastic. Try to find a positive angle to your message and put that first. A reader will not be receptive to the rest of the letter when you begin with negative factors. For instance, when turning down a credit application, tell the applicant what is positive about his credit record. Then explain why you cannot give him credit. If there's a possibility that he might be credit worthy in the future, conclude on this positive note. Even when your message is negative, say it with a smile.

In addition, you should convey your message with enthusiasm whenever possible. If you are not enthusiastic about your message, the reader won't be either. Your enthusiasm will be transferred to the reader when you are genuinely excited about the message and put that excitement in writing.

Be smooth and coherent. Each sentence and paragraph should follow logically from the previous one. The reader should not be left wondering how he got from one thought to the next. You get this result by organizing the letter before writing so you know exactly which points will be covered and in what order. Then work on the first and last sentence of each paragraph to make sure there are no jumps in logic.

Perk up your writing. Don't use jargon or unnecessary sentences. Avoid cliches, long phrases and flowery expressions. Write in correct, standard English, just the way you talk.

Put your message in short sentences and short paragraphs. You don't want the letter to look like it will be a burden to read. You also don't want the reader to get lost in a long paragraph when the same thoughts can be written in several short paragraphs.

"Proper" business letter writing style used to be so stilted and formal that you would often wonder why the writer bothered to put his alleged thoughts on paper. A dry, staid business letter would often contain nonsense clauses, like "In regard to the question at hand....", or "Our staff is taking your request under advisement, and will keep you posted as to any eventuality", or that old favorite, "If I can be of any further assistance, please don't hesitate to write". (Sure, buddy, but why weren't you of any assistance THIS time?)

The reason for this studied obfuscation ("conscious confusion") is that the First Law of Bureaucracy is to "cover your rear end", and many middle management letter writers assume this law translates into writing a letter so confusing as to say nothing, promise nothing, and thereby avoid legal liability for anything — either in a court of law, or in the boss's office.

Vanderbilt's Example

Writing in the *American Heritage* magazine, Peter Baida hearkened back to a famous letter by Cornelius Vanderbilt: "The excesses of contemporary business writing bring to mind my favorite business letter:"

Gentlemen:

You have undertaken to cheat me. I won't sue you, for the law is too slow. I'll ruin you.

Yours truly,
Cornelius Vanderbilt

"Not a word wasted", continued Baida. "If anyone can offer a better example of solid business writing, I would like to see it."

Modern businesspeople could learn a lesson from the brevity and clarity — if not the bravado and charity — of Vanderbilt's letter. Busy readers don't have time to wade through pointless paragraphs, or carefully worded verbal minefields, protecting one's rear guard.

The purpose of this book is to give you numerous examples of letters that work: guided missiles that land on target. As you take pen in hand (or dictaphone, typewriter, or computerized word processor), the pages of this book will provide open guidelines on adapting "styles that sell" to your own business situation.

How to Produce Impressive Letters

Writing is the most important part of a business letter, but it is not the only factor you should pay attention to. The appearance of your letter can have a dramatic effect on its success. The impact of your letter will be reduced if the message is presented in an unattractive format or produced on low-quality paper. Packaging counts. It's your letter's "body language". When the packaging is unattractive, the reader might ignore your letter or read it very skeptically.

Choose your stationery carefully. You don't need to buy the most expensive, embossed paper. In fact, often that will have an unfavorable impact on clients or customers. But you must use quality bond paper. Make sure the paper feels good to the hand and will reproduce characters and signatures clearly and permanently. You'll also want to be able to make corrections that are invisible to the average reader.

Paper generally is described by its weight, content, and grain. A paper's weight is the weight of 500 17″ x 22″ sheets. Standard business stationery is 20 pounds. More elegant stationery is 24 pounds, and paper for informal notes is 16 pounds.

The most expensive paper is made entirely from cotton fiber. Most paper, however, is a combination of wood and cotton fiber, with the cotton content varying between 25% and 75%. The grain is the direction of the fiber and is determined by the production process. Good stationery should have a grain that is parallel to the writing. Most stationery is 8-1/2″ x 11″, though shorter letters or personal notes can be written on smaller letterhead.

Your stationery also should have a letterhead printed on it. In most businesses, you don't need the more expensive engraved or raised letterhead. But you do need a clear, attractive design that projects the image you want the firm to have. Some businesses, particularly those associated with the arts, should have creative letterheads with colored paper and ink. Professionals, however, generally have very simple letterheads on white paper with black ink. The letterhead should contain the firm's name, address, and telephone number and often includes a brief description of its line of business as well as additional ways to contact the firm (telex, cable).

When a letter has more than one page, the subsequent sheets do not have a letterhead. They are plain sheets of the same color and quality as the letterhead.

Though envelopes are expensive, the envelope should be of the same quality and design as the letterhead. Some letter writers believe that envelopes are opened by a secretary and thrown away. Therefore, the reader never sees the envelope. But this practice is not universal, so you should not try to cut corners on envelopes.

How to Structure a Letter

Your letters should be typed or printed in a standard format and in a standard typeface. There are enough accepted formats to allow you some flexibility, but you should not use a format that is out of the ordinary. This will only distract the reader's attention from your message.

Every letter begins with a *heading*. Since your printed stationery contains the firm's name and address, the typed heading usually will contain only the current date. The date is centered, flush to the left, or flush to the right, depending on which letter format you use. The heading might also contain a *reference line*. The reference line identifies a letter which the reader previously sent to you or it contains either your account number or the number you are assigning to this letter.

Every letter should contain the recipient's name, title, firm, and address. This is known as the *inside address* and appears at least two lines below the heading. The inside address should be typed exactly as it appears on the reader's own letterhead or business card. Do not use abbreviations, other than Postal Service ZIP code abbreviations, unless it is necessary to keep a line from going past the center of the page.

Though the recipient's name is usually at the top of the inside address, some letters contain an *attention line* just below the inside address. The attention line usually reads: "Attention: Mr. John A. Doe." The attention line should be used only when you do not know the recipient personally or the relationship is purely a business one. Both the inside address and attention line are flush left.

Two spaces below the inside address and flush with the left margin is the *salutation*. The salutation generally reads "Dear Mr. Doe:" Always capitalize the first word of the salutation as well as any titles and names. The recipient's first name should be used in the salutation only when you know him or her well. Only titles that precede a name (Mr., Ms., Dr.) should be used in the salutation.

When you are unsure of who the recipient will be, the salutation can read "To whom it may concern," "Dear Sir or Madam," or something of that nature. The salutation should always be followed by a colon.

The salutation might be followed by a *subject line*. This device allows you to tell the reader quickly what the letter is about so that the first paragraph is not wasted on explanations. The subject line can be either centered or flush left. It generally starts with either "Subject:" or "Re." (Notice that a colon does not follow "Re.") You can write the subject line without these introductory words. If you do, be sure to underline the entire line.

You are now ready to type the *body of the letter*. The body can be single-spaced or double-spaced, though only short letters should be double-spaced. You should divide the body into paragraphs, with the first line of each paragraph either flush left or indented five to 10 spaces depending on the format you use. When a letter is double-spaced the first sentence of each paragraph should always be indented. When a letter is single-spaced you should double-space between paragraphs.

In a one-page letter the body should be centered on the page. In addition, the left and right margins should be at least one inch.

Two spaces below the body of the letter is the *complimentary close*. There are many options for the complimentary close (see chart) and you should select one that you are comfortable with. You might want to select several to use on different occasions. Only the first word of the closing is capitalized, and the closing is followed by a comma. The closing can be centered or flush left, depending on the format you have selected.

Your name should be typed four lines below the closing, and your *signature* should be made in the blank space. If you are signing for the firm in an official capacity, the firm's name should appear two lines below the closing. Your name should appear four lines below that.

Your title normally is typed either immediately after or below your name. This is optional, depending on your relationship to the reader and the image you want to convey.

Sometimes a secretary or other person signs letters for the writer. In such a case, the writer's name should be written in the normal signature space and the secretary's initials should be placed immediately below that.

The *identification initials* appear two lines below the writer's name and title and are flush left. The writer's initials are typed in all capitals, and the typist's or stenographer's initials are typed in lower case. A slash or colon usually separates the two sets of initials, i.e. RCC/ljw or RCC:ljw.

There are several accepted letter formats to choose from, and these are illustrated on the following pages. You can vary the styles somewhat to suit your tastes, but remember that the format should enhance your message, not direct attention away from it.

Selected Complimentary Closes

STANDARD CLOSES:	Sincerely, Sincerely yours, Yours sincerely,
FORMAL CLOSES:	Very truly yours, Yours truly, Yours very truly,
PROPER CLOSES:	Respectfully, Respectfully yours, Yours respectfully,
INFORMAL CLOSES:	Cordially, Cordially yours, Yours cordially,

A.B.C., Incorporated
One Main Street, U.S.A.
(555) 555-5555

DATE

INSIDE ADDRESS
XXXXXXXXXXXXXXXXXXXX
XXXXXXXXXXXXXXXXXX
XXXXXXXXXXXXXXXXXX

SALUTATION:

EVERY LINE, INCLUDING THE FIRST LINE OF EACH PARAGRAPH IS FLUSH LEFT.
XXXXXXXXXXXXXXXXXXXXXXXXXXXXXXXXXXXXXXXXXXXXXXXXXXXXXXXX
XXXXXXXXXXXXXXXXXXXXXXXXXXXXXXXXXXXXXXXXXXXXXXXXXXX

XXXXXXXXXXXXXXXXXXXXXXXXXXXXXXXXXXXXXXXXXXXXXXXXXXXXXXXX
XXXXXXXXXXXXXXXXXXXXXXXXXXXXXXXXXXXXXXXXXXXXXXXXXXXXX
XXXXXXXXXXXXXXXXXXXXXXXXXXXXXXXXXXXXXXXXXXXXXXXXXXXXX
XXXXXXXXXXXXXXXXXXXXXXXXXXXXXXXXXXXXXXXXXXXXXXXXXXXX
XXXXXXXXXXXXXXXXXXXXXXXXXXXXXXXXXXXXXXXXXXXXXXXXXXXX

XXXXXXXXXXXXXXXXXXXXXXXXXXXXXXXXXXXXXXXXXXXXXXXXXXXXXXXX
XXXXXXXXXXXXXXXXXXXXXXXXXXXXXXX

SALUTATION,

WRITER'S NAME
TITLE

IDENTIFICATION LINE

Block Style

A.B.C., Incorporated
One Main Street, U.S.A.
(555) 555-5555

THE DATE IS FLUSH RIGHT

AS IS THE REFERENCE LINE

THE INSIDE ADDRESS
IS FLUSH LEFT
XXXXXXXXXXXXXXXXXX
XXXXXXXXXXXXXXXXXX

SALUTATION:

IF THERE IS A SUBJECT LINE, IT IS FLUSH RIGHT. THE FIRST SENTENCE
OF EACH PARAGRAPH IS INDENTED.

THERE IS A DOUBLE SPACE BETWEEN EACH PARAGRAPH. XXXXXXXXXXX
XXXXXXXXXXXXXXXXXXXXXXXXXXXXXXXXXXXXXXXXXXXXXXXXXXXXX
XXXXXXXXXXXXXXXXXXXXXXXXXXXXXXXXXXXXXXXXXXXXXXXXXXXXX

THE COMPLIMENTARY CLOSING AND SIGNATURE ALSO ARE FLUSH RIGHT.
THE IDENTIFICATION LINE IS FLUSH LEFT.

SINCERELY,

WRITER'S NAME
TITLE

IDENTIFICATION LINE

Semi-Block Form #1

A.B.C., Incorporated
One Main Street, U.S.A.
(555) 555-5555

DATE

INSIDE ADDRESS
XXXXXXXXXXXXXXXXX
XXXXXXXXXXXXXXX
XXXXXXXXXXXXXXXXXXX

SALUTATION:

THE DATE LINE IS FLUSH LEFT IN THIS SEMI-BLOCK FORM. THE ONLY ITEMS THAT WOULD BE FLUSH RIGHT ARE THE REFERENCE LINE AND SUBJECT LINE.

PARAGRAPHS ARE INDENTED AND HAVE A DOUBLE SPACE BETWEEN THEM.

THE CLOSING AND SIGNATURE ON THIS FORM ARE CENTERED.

COMPLIMENTARY CLOSING,

NAME
TITLE

IDENTIFICATION LINE

Semi-Block Form #2

A.B.C., Incorporated
One Main Street, U.S.A.
(555) 555-5555

DATE LINE
INSIDE ADDRESS
XXXXXXXXXX
XXXXXXXXXXXX

SALUTATION:

    THE DATE LINE STARTS AT THE CENTER OF THE PAGE, AND THE ADDRESS IS IMMEDIATELY BELOW IT. EACH LINE IS INDENTED FIVE SPACES FROM THE LINE ABOVE.

    AN ALTERNATIVE IS TO PUT THE DATE LINE FLUSH RIGHT. THE INSIDE ADDRESS THEN STARTS FLUSH LEFT AND EACH LINE IS INDENTED FIVE SPACES FROM THE PREVIOUS LINE.

    THE REST OF THE LETTER IS THE SAME AS THE SEMI-BLOCK FORMAT #2.

CLOSING,

NAME
TITLE

IDENTIFICATION LINE

Indented Form

Hiring Employees

Business letters often become binding legal contracts. Most employees do not have formal written contracts, so the letter offering employment serves as the legal employment contract.

Offers of employment, therefore, must be carefully written. First, you want to be sure that all statements in the letter are clear, because any unclear statements are construed against the person who writes the contract. Second, the letter should cover all major conditions of the employment since you want employees concentrating on their jobs. Neither you nor the employee should waste time on the job ironing out issues that should have been resolved before the employee started work. In addition, even if such disputes are resolved fairly, the conflict almost certainly will result in some bad feelings and mutual suspicions on both sides.

Ideally an employment offer is written or at least reviewed by a lawyer, but small businesses can rarely justify this cost. When the offer is not reviewed by an attorney, the business should be careful to consider all the issues and policies that might arise about the job and clearly resolve those matters in the letter.

The letter should not contain legal terms unless it is written or reviewed by an attorney. Use basic English words and expressions that make your meaning clear to anyone reading the document.

Most of the business letters in this book are brief and to-the-point. Employment offers are different. Everything relevant to the job should be discussed and nothing should be assumed. The letter writer should be planning for the possibility that the letter could be the focus of litigation or arbitration involving the employee's salary or benefits.

The following terms occur frequently in employment offers or contracts:
- annual gross salary
- frequency of payment (monthly, semimonthly, etc.)
- formulas and payment schedules for bonuses and commissions
- fringe benefits, including pension and profit-sharing plans
- whether the individual is an employee or independent contractor

- expense-sharing agreements for independent contractors
- vacation time
- length of contract
- termination provisions, including notice and severance pay
- covenants not to compete or reveal trade secrets
- stock options
- definitions of special or technical terms

The provisions for the length of the contract and termination of the relationship are becoming more important. Most employment is "at will," meaning either party can terminate the contract at any time. A two-week notice period developed as a common courtesy, but it is not a legal requirement.

Lately, however, a number of court decisions are chipping away at "at will" employment agreements. Fired employees are winning large damage judgments for improper dismissals. These employees generally claim that they were victims of illegal discrimination based on sex, race, handicap, or age. In states with high unemployment, some courts are siding with employees and ruling that a job is an employee's right unless the employer can document specific reasons why the employee's performance was unsatisfactory.

The best defense against such suits is to have a personnel manual with specific job descriptions. The manual should detail how the employee's performance will be judged and what will be considered satisfactory. Periodic, written evaluations must be made and discussed with the employee.

This chapter contains letters describing the more common employment arrangements. If you have any creative agreements, the letters here can be used as models to develop effective employment offers.

JOB OFFERS

The letter you write to an employee offering him or her a job is an important one, not only because it details the parameters of the job and its compensation, but because it can actually be used as the employee agreement between yourself and the new employee. We have provided five versions of job offers: (1) Offering a Salaried Job on a Biweekly Basis, (2) Offering a Job and Including Noncompetition and Trade Secret Provisions, (3) Offering a Job with a Bonus Provision, (4) Offering a Job with Employee and Employer Splitting Profits, and (5) Offering a Job with Stock Options. These examples are just that, examples, and should be used as cut-and-paste references in order for you to develop an offer appropriate for your situation.

Tips on How to Customize Your Letters:

1. In all cases, you can take two different opening approaches. One, a friendly welcome, or two, an official confirmation. It depends on your situation, personality, and distance from the new employee as to which tone you take to open your letter.

2. The most important thing to remember in these letters is to include every and all facts pertinent to the job itself. Financial facts are extremely important to spell out to avoid misunderstanding and conflicts later on. The clearer your letter, the better you understand each other, and the better your business relationship starts off.

3. Close your letter with an encouraging remark about his or her qualifications if you opened with a welcome.

4. If you opened with an official confirmation, close the letter with a specific instruction as to the amount of time the offer will be held open and how you want to see the acceptance.

5. In all cases, if you plan to use this letter as your official employment agreement, make sure to have the employee sign and date a copy. Send one copy with both your and the employee's signature to your lawyer, keep one in your personnel files.

Optional Paragraphs and Phrases:

• Welcome to ABC Industries! We may be a little premature in our enthusiasm for you to accept our offer of employment in the position of production manager.

• This letter confirms our telephone discussion of _____, whereby you were offered the position of production clerk at a weekly salary of _____.

• Although you will be receiving an Employee Manual with a full description of all company policies and procedures upon acceptance of this offer, we thought we might outline the most important facts about your job in particular:

• Attached please find a list of company benefits and a complete job description for the position of Production Clerk. This offer is based on your understanding and acceptance of both these items.

- You will be pleased to know that over 100 people applied for the position we are offering you, but obviously we feel that you are by far the best qualified person for the job. We offer our congratulations for that accomplishment.

- The terms of this offer are as follows:

- Your employment, should you accept this offer, will begin on _____ , at a starting salary of _____ , and will continue until one of us decides otherwise giving two weeks notice.

- We are a growing organization with many benefits and opportunities to offer our employees. We certainly hope you agree with our feeling that you and ABC Industries will make a perfect match.

- Please sign the enclosed three copies of this letter. Keep one for your records and return the other two in the enclosed postage-paid envelope.

- We will provide you with all materials, supplies and equipment necessary for performance of your duties. In addition, you will be provided an office and secretary on our premises and at our expense.

- All our employees serve a three-month probationary period at the beginning of their employment. During probation, you will not participate in benefit programs and will receive written evaluations monthly. An employee on probation can be terminated at any time during the period. After successful completion of the probationary period, you will fully participate in all benefit programs retroactively and can be terminated only upon two weeks written notice.

- This job will require a substantial amount of travel at times. All reasonable travel expenses will be paid by us, and you will be reimbursed for all out-of-pocket expenses upon presentation of appropriate receipts. The travel is an integral part of the job and cannot be refused without our permission. We will try to relieve you of travel responsibilities when there is a good reason, such as personal illness or family emergency.

- Part of the equipment provided for you will be a company car selected by us and an oil company credit card. We will pay all maintenance and operating costs of the vehicle. Because of the new tax law, you will have to keep an accurate log of all mileage and expenses. Personal mileage must be included in your gross income at the Internal Revenue Service's standard mileage rate. Failure to keep records that will satisfy our tax accountant will cause us to lose substantial tax benefits for which you will have to reimburse us, if we so choose.

- All of our employees are subject to the rules and regulations contained in our company personnel manual, which you will be given on your first day of work. You can review a copy of the manual at our offices any time before then.

- This offer is conditioned upon verification of your references and all items on your resume. This offer and any subsequent employment relationship will be terminated immediately, without notice or severance pay, if any of these items cannot be satisfactorily verified.

• All copyrights or patents obtained on items made in the course of your employment here or made through the use of the firm's facilities and equipment shall be our property. You can obtain such copyrights or patents in your own name but must immediately assign all rights to the firm.

• As a condition of your employment you agree not to engage in a competitive business within a 100-mile radius of our headquarters, in your own name or under any other, for one full year after termination of the employment relationship.

A.B.C., Incorporated
One Main Street, U.S.A.
(555) 555-5555

Dear   :

    We are pleased to offer you a position as assistant
bookkeeper.

    The position pays $ per month, which is paid in equal
increments every other Friday. In addition, you will receive two
weeks' paid vacation every 12 months, health insurance benefits
and $10,000 of life insurance.

    This job is on a two-week basis, which means that either
party can terminate the relationship upon giving two weeks'
written notice to the other party.

    We were very pleased with the quality of the applicants for
this job and believe you will be an outstanding addition to our
firm. If you have any questions about the position or the firm,
call me at any time.

                            Sincerely,

                            John Smith

                            John Smith

*Job offer — salaried job on
a biweekly basis*

A.B.C., Incorporated
One Main Street, U.S.A.
(555) 555-5555

Dear   :

   On the basis of our recent discussion, we hereby offer you the position of assistant to the president with the following terms and conditions:

   1.   The position pays $25,000 per year, payable biweekly in equal installments.

   2.   Fringe benefits include two weeks' paid vacation (scheduled at the convenience of the employer) and participation in our employee benefit programs. Current benefits include health insurance, life insurance, a pension plan and profit sharing. Programs may be added or discontinued at any time.

   3.   The employee agrees not to engage in any other occupation or business during the term of his employment but will devote his full time and abilities to furthering the interests of the employer.

   4.   As assistant to the president, the employee will have access to the trade secrets, business plans and production processes of the employer. The employee covenants to keep such information confidential and not to aid any individual or business that is a competitor or potential competitor of the employer. The employee further covenants not to compete, either in his own name or with another business, against the employer for a period of one year after termination of his employment.

   5.   The employee agrees to work for the employer for two years or until the employer terminates this agreement by giving 30 days' written notice.

   This offer shall remain open for two weeks from the date above. Acceptance of this offer must be in writing.

                              Sincerely,

                              John Smith

                              John Smith

A.B.C., Incorporated
One Main Street, U.S.A.
(555) 555-5555

Dear   :

    We are pleased to offer you the position of list manager
with our direct mail firm.

    The job carries a salary of $20,000. In addition, there is
an incentive bonus of 5 percent of the net profits from list
rentals above $50,000. Net profits are determined by subtracting
the direct costs of list rental from the gross revenues. Direct
costs are salaries (including employment taxes and fringe
benefits), long distance telephone charges, postage, shipping
charges, and computer expenses. Office overhead expenses are not
part of direct costs. Federal and state income taxes are not
subtracted from gross revenues in computing the bonus.

    This agreement will run for two years from the date you
start working for us. Either party can terminate the agreement
upon two weeks' written notice.

    We think you will find this agreement attractive.

                              Sincerely,

                              John Smith

Job offer — with bonus provision

A.B.C., Incorporated
One Main Street, U.S.A.
(555) 555-5555

Dear   :

After interviewing numerous candidates, we are glad to offer
you the job of assistant manager at ABC, Incorporated.

The starting salary is $15,000. In addition, the assistant
manager shares in all net profits above $50,000 each year as
follows. All officers and employees share in 25 percent of the
net profits above $50,000. Only full-time employees who have
been employed for the prior 12 months share in the profits. Each
eligible employee receives a pro rata portion of the profits
according to the ratio his gross salary bears to the total gross
salaries of all eligible officers and employees. The amount of
net profits is determined by our accountants according to generally accepted accounting principles.

The bonus payments are determined and paid within ten days
after the accountants prepare the annual statements. If the
employment agreement is terminated during the year, the
employee's share of the bonus is prorated for the period of
employment.

This agreement will run for three years from the date you
begin working for us. Either party may terminate the employment
relationship on two weeks' written notice.

We are a growing firm and believe in hiring employees who
will be motivated by an incentive plan such as this. We believe
you are such an individual and look forward to having you with
us.

Sincerely,

John Smith

John Smith

*Job offer — with employer and
employee splitting profits*

A.B.C., Incorporated
One Main Street, U.S.A.
(555) 555-5555

Dear   :

This letter is to confirm the agreement we reached regarding your employment as our general manager.

Your employment will start on March 1, 19 , and run for three years. During this period you will devote your entire time and attention to the business and will perform the tasks and duties assigned to you by the company president or the Board of Directors.

The salary for the job will be $45,000 annually, paid in equal increments on the first of each month. In addition, you will participate in our employee benefits under the rules already established for those programs and receive two weeks of paid vacation.

As further compensation, we are granting you the option to purchase 100 shares of our Class A common stock at the end of each full year of your employment. To exercise this option, you must submit written notice to that effect to the corporate secretary between February 15 and March 1, accompanied by payment of $7.50 for each share you wish to purchase.

Failure to exercise the option in one year shall not affect the option to purchase stock in a subsequent year. Unexercised options expire and cannot be exercised in a subsequent year. Further, the options are personal to you and cannot be assigned or transferred in any way. All stock purchased shall carry any restrictions voted on the Class A common stock by the Board of Directors.

This agreement may be terminated by us upon 30 days' written notice and payment of one month's salary.

Please confirm this agreement by signing in the space indicated and returning the original to us. A copy is enclosed for your records.

Sincerely,

John Smith

John Smith

Confirmed, accepted and agreed to,

_____
Name   Date

Job offer — with stock options

REJECTING EMPLOYMENT APPLICATIONS — SOLICITED AND UNSOLICITED

Keep in mind that an applicant who does not fit into your organization right now may be just who you are looking for a few years from now. Try to turn down the applicant and still leave him or her with a positive feeling about the company and him or herself. Of course, you will want to give a little extra care to those applicants you sought out. After all, you saw enough merit in them originally to ask them to apply, so the chances that you may want to recontact them are greater than they are for unsolicited applicants.

Tips on How to Customize Your Letters:

1. Thank the applicant for taking the time to apply.

2. Assure the person that his or her application was seriously considered.

3. Try to avoid dwelling on any particular failing or lack of qualities on the part of the applicant.

4. Wish the applicant luck and keep the letter on an upbeat note.

Optional Paragraphs and Phrases:

• Thank you for your resume and letter in response to our ad in the Main Street Chronicle.

• We appreciate your taking the time to let us know your qualifications and that you are available for employment. Unfortunately at this time, our organization does not have any openings.

• You made our decision a difficult one. Your qualifications and experience are excellent. Unfortunately, there was another candidate with just a little more experience in a field more closely related to our firm.

• Please accept our best wishes for success in your career endeavors.

• We will definitely be keeping your resume and application on file. If another position opens up, or our chosen candidate does not work out, we will positively be in touch with you.

• Thank you for expressing an interest in our firm. Such interest from qualified people like you is a great compliment to our firm.

• We spent a great deal of time thoroughly analyzing the candidates and were forced to make many difficult decisions.

• A surprising number of people responded to our notice, and this made competition for the position especially keen. We regret being able to hire only one of the applicants.

• We would like to consider you for future vacancies and will retain your resume in our files.

• You are a highly qualified candidate and were one of the finalists for this position. I'm sure you will find something similar with no trouble.

A.B.C., Incorporated
One Main Street, U.S.A.
(555) 555-5555

Dear   :

    After considerable debate about our needs, we decided to offer the assistant manager position to someone else. Our offer was accepted, so the position now is filled.

    We enjoyed talking with you and felt that you could add a number of fresh and creative ideas to our firm and would work well with our present staff. The candidate we selected, however, has considerable hands-on experience in management at operations similar to ours. We believe this experience is more important to our firm at this time.

    Thank you for the time and ideas you gave us and keep in touch. I am sure you will find a suitable position in the near future, and I will do whatever I can to help.

                  Sincerely,

                  John Smith

                  John Smith

*Letter rejecting solicited
employment application*

A.B.C., Incorporated
One Main Street, U.S.A.
(555) 555-5555

Dear   :

    Thank you for your recent letter and your interest in ABC Company.

    We have reviewed your letter and resume and compared them to our recent needs. Unfortunately, we have no openings now or in the foreseeable future for someone with your qualifications and interests. We will keep your resume on hand in case this situation should unexpectedly change.

    We appreciate your interest in the firm and wish you the best of luck in your search.

                Sincerely,

                John Smith

Letter rejecting unsolicited employment application

LETTER OF REFERENCE FOR FORMER EMPLOYEE

Choose your words carefully when writing this letter. The Fair Employment Practice prohibits employers from writing anything negative about former employees. The best way to protect yourself is to offer only facts, or better yet confirm facts that the prospective new employer offers you. Stick to whether or not the employee did work for you, for what time period, and what the position entailed. If you were satisfied with the employee and he or she left on good terms, you may want to offer a comment about the quality of work.

Tips on How to Customize Your Letter:

1. First paragraphs should contain all the pertinent facts.

2. You may then want to add a small amount about the quality of work. (Again we recommend doing this only if you have something positive to say.)

3. You may want to consider offering additional information. If not, close by saying that your company's policy is to furnish only the above facts.

Optional Paragraphs and Phrases:

• In response to your request for a reference on _____. He was employed by ABC Industries from _____ to _____, in the position of _____.

• To answer your request for a reference on _____, it is our company policy to only confirm facts about employment and offer no subjective opinions. Please send us a list of facts you wish to have confirmed, and we will be happy to do so.

• We would like to be able to help you more, but our company policy only allows us to confirm employment, the time interval, and position.

• Thank you for thinking of us in this matter.

• We recognized at once that he is a quick learner and could master new functions and tasks with little trouble.

• Linda actively sought new responsibilities and handled them well. She initiated several policies that have improved our operation markedly.

A.B.C., Incorporated
One Main Street, U.S.A.
(555) 555-5555

Dear   :

    Genevieve McGough was employed with our firm as assistant
production manager from July 15, 19 , through August 22, 19 .
She left the firm to accept a better position.

    During her employment here we were very satisfied with her
work. In addition to performing her regular duties well, she
frequently worked overtime without complaint.

    If you need additional information, just let me know.

                Sincerely,

                John Smith

                John Smith

Letter of reference for
former employee

REQUEST FOR EMPLOYMENT REFERENCE

This can be a very standard letter. In fact it might be a good one to put on your word processor. Simply ask for a reference and explain the details you are looking for.

Tips on How to Customize Your Letter:

1. Give the applicant's name and the position he or she is applying for in the first sentence.

2. Explain why you are approaching this particular firm.

3. Give the details of your request.

4. Then, of course, thank the reader for his or her help.

Optional Paragraphs and Phrases:

• _____, who we understand was formerly employed by your firm has applied for the position of _____ here at ABC Industries.

• Would you please give us a reference on this candidate?

• The information we are interested in is as follows:
   — Job description
   — Dates of employment with your company
   — Performance evaluation
   — Reason for leaving your company

• If you have any problems with furnishing us with these items, please let us know.

• Let us know if you want us to keep your reference confidential.

• Thank you in advance for your time and cooperation.

A.B.C., Incorporated
One Main Street, U.S.A.
(555) 555-5555

Dear   :

    We have received an application for employment from
                       , seeking a position with our firm in the
capacity of   . We understand the applicant was
previously employed by your firm.

    Accordingly, we would appreciate a reference on the
individual, including confirmation of the dates of employment
with you, job description, performance evaluation, and reasons
for termination.

    Please advise whether your reference should be held
confidential.

    Thank you for your anticipated cooperation.

                 Sincerely,

                 John Smith

                 John Smith

Request for employment reference

WAIVER OF CONFIDENTIALITY

Whenever information about an employee is requested, have the employee sign a letter waiving his or her right to confidentiality before releasing the information. Often, wage or personal information is requested by welfare agencies, spouses or other parties. Release of this information without the signed letter from the employee could result in an invasion of privacy action.

Tips on How to Customize Your Letter:

1. Make this letter have more of a legal tone.

2. Keep it short.

3. Include all pertinent information, especially: who is asking for the information, what the information is, and the date.

Optional Paragraphs and Phrases:

• I, in the form of this letter, give my employer _____ permission to release the following information to _____ who has requested it.

• I understand that _____ has requested access to my personal file at _____ .

• I give _____ my permission to show my records to _____ for reasons of _____ .

A.B.C., Incorporated
One Main Street, U.S.A.
(555) 555-5555

I, the undersigned employee, acknowledge that my employer has received a request from   for certain information relating to my employment.

I hereby grant my employer full permission to provide the information described as:

_____
Employee

Waiver of confidentiality

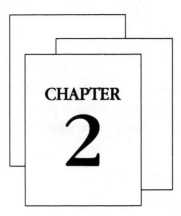

CHAPTER

2

Building Employee Morale

Building goodwill with employees is as important as building goodwill with customers. Often an expression of appreciation to an employee is as effective as a few extra dollars in the paycheck. A personal letter that the employee can take home or that is put in his personnel file brings excellent results.

An employee goodwill letter should be written whenever an employee does a particularly good job on a project or does more than the job calls for. Valuable suggestions, overtime work and exceeding goals are good subjects for these letters. The effect of introducing new fringe benefits also can be maximized by sending personal letters to employees.

If employee goodwill letters are used, they should be used consistently. Too often a firm will try to stimulate or encourage a particular employee with goodwill letters and not send letters to other employees achieving similar accomplishments. This practice has the opposite of the intended effect because other employees become discouraged.

LETTER RECOGNIZING A SUGGESTION

Good suggestions and ideas from employees are the business owner's single most valuable source for growth. One sure way to keep good suggestions coming is to reinforce the employees who make them. And an excellent way to reinforce this valuable brain work is to write the employee a letter.

Tips on How to Customize Your Letter:

1. Mention the idea or suggestion immediately. It's a good idea to have it written in the letter for documentation sake.

2. If you plan to use the suggestion, say how. If not, mention that you may in the future.

3. Be sincere and generous with the expression of your appreciation.

4. If appropriate, state how submitting the suggestion will help the employee as well as the company.

Optional Paragraphs and Phrases:

• Thank you for your suggestion on the newsletter renewal self-mailer.

• It will save the company an enormous amount of money and will be attractive to our customers as well. As a result, we are planning on implementing it this month.

• Unfortunately our mailing plan for the year has been completed, and we can find no money in the budget to test your idea. You can rest assured, however, that as soon as we enter the new fiscal year, your idea will be implemented.

• I want you to understand how much you have done for the company by offering us your idea. We are truly appreciative.

• Management believes that your recent suggestion is superb. You've solved a problem that we've been working on for some time.

• This is the kind of creativity that higher-paid personnel are supposed to come up with. Therefore, we are enclosing a check for $750 with this letter.

• Your idea is one we considered in the past and once had great hope for. There are several significant problems, however, that are not readily apparent.

• It will take us some time to evaluate this idea. In the meantime I wanted you to know that suggestions are encouraged and yours is being considered very carefully.

A.B.C., Incorporated
One Main Street, U.S.A.
(555) 555-5555

Dear   :

It is my pleasure to commend you for the suggestion to change our purchasing methods. We have thoroughly reviewed your suggestion and believe that the firm can save both time and money by taking bids under the system you described. We will be implementing this idea soon.

We greatly appreciate the time and thought you put into this idea. We try to encourage this kind of initiative and hope you will continue to look for ways to improve our operations and submit your ideas to the management.

A copy of this letter is being placed in your file as a permanent part of your employment record.

Sincerely,

John Smith

John Smith

Letter recognizing a suggestion

LETTER OF ENCOURAGEMENT

You may think that an annual raise or an occasional promotion is enough to let an employee know he or she is doing a good job. Wrong! Employees need to hear from their supervisors, and especially from the owner of a company, that they are valuable to the company. A letter of encouragement, even if it is to the whole staff, will do wonders for morale and productivity. Sometimes managers/owners send a letter of this type to coincide with announcement of upcoming events.

Tips on How to Customize Your Letter:

1. Show how much your employees mean to you.

2. Indicate strongly that you believe that the company's greatest resource is its people.

3. If you discuss upcoming events, make their significance to the employees clear.

Optional Paragraphs and Phrases:

(Some of these are if, unlike the sample, you are writing to just one employee.)

• I would like you to attend our annual summer picnic. Attendance isn't required, of course, but I've found that it is good for co-workers to see each other away from the office periodically.

• I want to offer personal thanks for the outstanding work you've done the last few weeks. When you came on board, I promised that there would not be much overtime work. But as you know we've had an emergency recently, and I appreciate your cooperation during this period.

• To reward employees for this year's excellent results, we are going to close the office and give everyone an unscheduled three-day weekend.

• I'm very grateful for the way everyone performed during the recent hard times. I assure you that when we have completed this turnaround employees will be amply rewarded.

• As you know from rumors in the industry, "everyone" is having a disastrous year in sales. Except us, that is. And much of that credit goes to your personal sales efforts.

• In our monthly top management "brainstorm" sessions, it struck all of us on the Board of Directors that we're not yet fully utilizing your unique talents in the company.

• This is the third anniversary of your joining our company, and I've made a preliminary tally of your bottom-line profit production. Enclosed find my enthusiastic "thank you" in the form of a 10% annual salary increase and bonus.

• As you know, I don't have much time to read the industry press any more. Your constant review of these sources—on your own time, no less—is of great value to me. Keep up the good work and "keep those clippings coming".

- Your thorough evaluation of the pending contract was an eye-opener to me. It's forced me to re-evaluate my opinion of our legal firm. (Why didn't *they* catch the obvious "loopholes" you caught?) From now on, I'll forward other legal matters to you for a similar careful analysis.

- I notice your car here every Saturday morning as I drive by on my way to the golf course. Your excellent work reflects the long hours of unpaid overtime you're working. This little bonus says, "Good job. Keep it up".

- After just 45 days of your 90-day probation as a new employee, I've decided to waive the 90 days and welcome you aboard as a bona-fide full time employee, eligible for all company benefits.

- I wonder if you and your wife are free the weekend of July 15 to accompany my wife and me on a two-day sailing excursion in the Bahamas. I look forward to getting to know both of you, as key employees and as friends.

- Your work on the Harvey account was excellent. Their half-million dollars in annual business will boost our profits by 10% immediately. As a partial reward, I'm turning the lucrative Holland account over to your "stable" of customers.

A.B.C., Incorporated
One Main Street, U.S.A.
(555) 555-5555

Dear   :

    I would like to take this opportunity to update a few items for you.

    The growth we have experienced this past year has exceeded our goals. By the end of the fiscal year, our sales should exceed $. We believe much of this unexpected growth is due to the increased productivity and enthusiasm of our employees, and we want to thank you for doing your part.

    We have several plans for the near future that should continue this growth. A new store is currently planned for the   . We are considering several sites and plan to have the store open for business within the next six months. Current employees will be given a preference for management and other positions at the new location, and we want each of you to think about applying for these positions. Full job descriptions should be available within 90 days.

    The next year should present exciting challenges and opportunities for our firm. We hope you will fully participate in these events.

                Sincerely,

                John Smith

Letter of encouragement

LETTER TO NEW EMPLOYEE

Outside of the application and interviewing process, the first impression a new employee may have of you and your firm is this letter. And we all know how important first impressions are to lasting relationships. If you use the Job Offer Letters in the previous chapter to discuss salary, benefits, and job responsibilities, you are left free to use this letter as a true welcome effort.

Tips on How to Customize Your Letter:

1. Express your pleasure in the person becoming a member of your staff.

2. Include any information you may have left out of the Job Offer Letter. Or if you did not send a letter to extend the offer, incorporate that material here.

3. Give a little pitch for the company as well. Reinforce the reader's decision to accept the job.

Optional Paragraphs and Phrases:

• It is our pleasure to welcome you to the ABC, Inc. family.

• September 15 will be a busy day for both of us, so let me extend my official welcome now. We can then be more relaxed on the 15th.

• ABC has grown so much over the past few years. We know you will enjoy all the opportunities you will encounter here, just as we will enjoy the great contributions you will be making to the company.

• Please report for work at the ABC Company on April 10. You should first report to work at the personnel office at 9:00 a.m.

• I'm happy to welcome you to our firm. Your career at ABC will begin with orientation in the personnel office on April 10 at 9:00 a.m.

• The more you learn about this industry, the more you will realize that we are very well respected by both our customers and competitors.

• We think you will fill a gap in our firm and that we will all profit from this association.

• You will be given responsibility and authority as soon as you can handle it. I know this is what you want, so I think you'll enjoy working here.

A.B.C., Incorporated
One Main Street, U.S.A.
(555) 555-5555

Dear   :

     We are looking forward to your arrival here on September 15.
We're glad to have you joining our staff.

     You are now part of a growing publishing company of quality
business manuals and tax guides. Our products have been well
received by thousands of businesses and professionals. Since we
talked, we have decided to introduce the new publications we were
considering. You will play a large role in the success of these
products.

     Again, welcome to the firm. If there is anything we can do
between now and the 15th, please let me know.

                                        Sincerely,

                                        John Smith

                                        John Smith

Letter to new employee

ANNOUNCING A PROMOTION

This is one of those letters that is just completely fun and pleasurable to write. It is important that promotions are announced by letter as well as verbally in order that the employee's file is well documented.

Tips on How to Customize Your Letter:

1. Explain that the employee was given the promotion on the merit of his or her work.

2. Congratulate the employee.

3. Be sincere and casual in the tone of your letter.

Optional Paragraphs and Pharases:

• You have shown such ability and growth in the past year, that we are happy to promote you from Assistant Editor to Editor.

• Congratulations on your accomplishment this year and on this promotion. We are very proud to have you as an employee.

• It has only been three months, but your work has been so outstanding that we feel it is appropriate to promote you from Traffic Manager to Company Purchasing Agent. Congratulations!

• We've reached a consensus on who should be our new marketing director, and we've decided it should be you.

• You are aware of the amount of time we spent on this decision, so you must know that there were many excellent candidates for the position.

• The only regret I have about this promotion is that you no longer will be available to assist me.

A.B.C., Incorporated
One Main Street, U.S.A.
(555) 555-5555

Dear   :

    We have carefully evaluated all the applicants and are
pleased to offer you the job of assistant production manager.

    A number of qualified people applied for this position, but
you were unquestionably the top candidate. We have benefited
substantially from your past efforts at the firm and believe you
can accomplish even more in this position.

    Congratulations. You deserve this opportunity.

                                Sincerely,

                                John Smith

                                John Smith

SYMPATHY LETTER TO AN EMPLOYEE

If an employee suffers any personal loss or injury, it is a thoughtful gesture for you, the employer, to offer your sympathies in the form of a letter.

Tips on How to Customize Your Letter:

1. Make your letter brief, but sincere.

2. Don't be overly emotional, but let the employee know you care.

3. Let the employee know you are there to support him or her and offer your assistance in any way.

Optional Paragraphs and Phrases:

- I just found out yesterday evening that your mother has passed away. Please accept my deepest sympathies.

- I heard about your automobile accident over the weekend. What a horrible experience. I certainly hope you recover very soon.

- Please don't worry about anything at work. We have it under control, which is not to say that we don't miss you!

- I hope you realize that if you need anything at all, I am here to ask.

- Please let us know if there is anything we can do to ease the pain.

- Hurry back!

- Let me offer my deepest sympathies on your recent loss.

- The loss of a family member is always distressing, even when it was expected and we thought we were prepared for it.

- I know that nothing I can say or do will ease your sorrow. But I want you to know that my thoughts are with you.

- Please accept the sincere sympathy of everyone here and let us know if there is any way we can help.

- We'd like to add our sincere condolences about your loss. Many people at the firm knew your wife well and will miss her deeply.

A.B.C., Incorporated
One Main Street, U.S.A.
(555) 555-5555

Dear   :

    I was sorry to hear that you are in the hospital. I am told
that your illness is not serious, so I hope that you are feeling
well by the time this letter reaches you.

    The tasks that would require your immediate attention are
being handled by several other people. But needless to say, we
miss you - both personally and professionally - and are looking
forward to your speedy recovery.

                  Sincerely,

                  John Smith

                  John Smith

Sympathy letter to an employee

ANNOUNCING NEW FRINGE BENEFITS

A written announcement of a new employee benefit program or additions to the existing one is the most effective efficient manner in which to handle the situation. Employees can take their time to study the letter, and you can cut back on extensive meeting time.

Tips on How to Customize Your Letter:

1. State the effective date and to whom it applies in the first paragraph.

2. Explain the details clearly and completely.

3. Be sure to emphasize throughout your explanation how the program and/or additions will truly benefit the employee.

4. You may want to have the details drawn up in a brochure if the changes or new plans are extensive.

Optional Paragraphs and Phrases:

• We have added two important features to our medical plan, effective January 1 of next year.

• To ease the burden on our working parents, we have decided to add daycare facilities to our organization.

• We believe that our new profit-sharing plan will allow us all to grow rich together. Since all employees now are shareholders in the business, each of you benefits directly from cost reductions and profit increases.

• Our survey indicates that dental costs are the biggest health care expense for most of you. We've also found that these costs can be reduced significantly by the establishment of a group dental insurance plan.

• Your rights and responsibilities under this plan are rather extensive and complicated. Therefore we strongly urge you to read the enclosed brochure *and* attend the orientation meeting next week. This meeting is being held on the premises on company time.

• Sometimes employees don't realize exactly how much fringe benefits such as these are worth. This plan alone costs the firm $84 a month per employee. And this is much cheaper than you could buy the same benefits as an individual.

• Because of changes in the tax law, certain fringe benefits now are taxable to employees. We are restructuring our benefit plans to avoid this treatment as much as possible, but some of you will be subject to additional withholding taxes despite our efforts.

A.B.C., Incorporated
One Main Street, U.S.A.
(555) 555-5555

Dear   :

We are pleased to announce that ABC Company is establishing a pension plan effective January 1. The plan covers all full-time employees and is funded entirely with employer contributions.

The new pension plan is fully explained in the enclosed brochure, but I will discuss the highlights in this letter.

All full-time employees with at least three years of service will have contributions made on their behalf at the end of each fiscal year. The contributions are fully vested when made. This means that if you leave the firm for any reason, you can take the value of the pension account with you. Contributions will be a percentage of your salary, and the percentage depends on your gross income. A schedule of pension contributions is on Page 11 of the brochure.

You will have to designate a beneficiary of your account just as you do for our group life insurance plan. Please complete the beneficiary designation form on Page 15 of the brochure and return it to me before January 1.

Study the enclosed brochure carefully. On November 15 a representative from a pension consulting firm will be at the office to explain the plan and answer any questions you have. The meeting will be held during working hours, and everyone is invited.

The pension plan is another milestone in our firm's continued growth. We believe that our employees play a significant part in that growth, and we want to encourage enthusiasm and commitment in our employees. This is just another step in our program to reward our employees for their fine performance.

Sincerely,

John Smith

John Smith

MEMO EXPLAINING THE COMPANY'S POSITION AND POLICY

Every now and then a situation will require a policy or procedure to be explained and clarified. The best way to accomplish this is in writing.

Tips on How to Customize Your Letter:

1. State the situation precipitating the explanation.

2. State the policy being explained and reinforced.

3. Be clear and to the point.

4. Show how the policy helps the employees as well as the company.

5. End the memo with a reassuring message.

6. This information should be in a memo format to be easily added to an employee handbook.

Optional Paragraphs and Phrases:

• It has been brought to my attention that the profit sharing plan has never been adequately explained to our staff.

• Our vacation policy is as follows:

• Company procedure as far as ordering supplies is concerned is that all purchases must be made with the approval of the purchasing agent.

• This will help to ensure that everyone receives their supplies in a timely manner and the company is not overspending.

• Some of you are confused about our new policy on company cars. This policy is a bit complicated and was required by the new tax law, so I am circulating this memo to explain the policy.

• As you know, we have been reviewing our purchasing procedures for some time. We have developed a new policy and will require its use immediately.

• Because of some inconsistencies in the past, all customer complaints now will be transferred to Nora Raim. If she is absent, she will designate the person to handle complaints.

• While we don't like to impose such rigid rules, in this case we have found that mistakes can be avoided only if the procedures we've developed are followed precisely.

A.B.C., Incorporated
One Main Street, U.S.A.
(555) 555-5555

TO: All Employees

FROM: President

SUBJECT: Policy

DATE:

    I am aware that various rumors are circulating about our financial position, so I believe it is essential that you receive a clear and candid statement of the facts and our planned strategies.

    As you know, we are experiencing a cash flow problem. This is due largely to an unexpected drop in sales. After talking with competitors and suppliers, we are convinced this is an industrywide recession and not due to any special shortcomings of our firm.

    Nevertheless, we do believe the firm can be more efficient and will be making some belt-tightening moves shortly. We also believe that personnel costs are already "lean and mean" and that our current staff is essential to our competing successfully in this tight market. Accordingly, we plan to keep all our personnel.

    The changes we will be making emphasize improved purchasing, better collections and reduction of overhead other than personnel. It is essential that each employee cooperate fully in implementing these new policies.

    We believe the current problems are temporary and that both the firm and industry will be profitable over the long term. If this letter does not clarify any issues that concern you, do not hesitate to ask me.

*Memo explaining the company's
position and policy*

CHAPTER

3

Building Careers

Many business people are sole proprietors of a small business, or a married couple with grown children operating a "Mom & Pop" company. This kind of cottage industry is considered by many observers to be the wave of the future, or "Megatrend" of the 1990s and beyond.

The business letters in the rest of this book are primarily devoted to small businesses with an employee base, a battery of customers and/or clients, a site of operation (outside the home), and widely recognized community status as a business. This chapter, however, deals primarily with those small businesses that operate on a sole proprietorship basis, or with just limited or part-time help.

A Career Building Letter is written with the sole purpose of landing a new client, or even a full-time job. It is far superior to a resume, in that it is tailored to the potential employer's (or client's) needs in the marketplace. You're not selling yourself as much as you are selling the results, or benefits, which your new client/employer can expect from you.

The concept of this type of letter came from *Executive Jobs Unlimited*, a book by Carl Boll. The concept was amplified in a later best-seller, *What Color is Your Parachute?* by Richard N. Bolles. It involves writing a personalized sales letter, preferably on a word-processing machine which can be programmed to adapt each letter to the specific target audience. This involves changing addresses and salutations, plus perhaps changing the body of the letter to fit each client's potential needs.

As the examples in this chapter will show, these letters are geared to hit the "hot button" of a potential client. The letters show how you can generate greater profits for the executive's company by cutting overhead, smoothing operations, bringing new customers, etc.

First, of course, you must make a searching inventory of your strongest business qualifications. Who cares about your previous title, salaries, employers, or education at this point? Your potential client surely doesn't care about these details, not at first anyway. He only cares about what you can do for his business, NOW.

The Career Building Letter is structured to put the key benefits up front, followed by a brief description of how you have brought that kind of benefit to previous companies, followed by specific proposal of work benefits for the client's company, or an opportunity to describe them in more detail in a private meeting.

A little familiarity with the company's products or service is vital, but it needn't be detailed knowledge in order to write a good letter. It's most important to *know yourself*, and what you can bring to the company. In your own personal analysis, look at your whole career in terms of a series of projects which either helped or hurt your employer on the bottom line. Learn from your mistakes, but then totally discard those mistakes from your research. *Isolate your triumphs*, and then describe them in terms of your employer's potential benefit.

Most people have neglected to make such a personal and business inventory of the strengths they bring to the marketplace, when a bold analysis of their value to a company can bring out many specific monetary benefits on the bottom line. The examples that follow will demonstrate this kind of analysis in action.

Always try to put a number on these triumphs of yours. QUANTIFY! Employers want to see bottom-line figures. If your contribution saved $10,000 on a contract, say so. If you did the job of two people, say it in numbers: "I saved the company $15,000 in extra salaries." If you serviced a leading customer, say you were "responsible for $1,000,000 in business".

Also look for comparisons. Compare your record to the employee who preceded you. Did you take a defunct department and make it a leader? Did you double the output or sales of your predecessor? Did you expand production with the same staff? Did you cut loss of time due to sickness or accidents? All of these success stories have numbers associated with them, so speak the universal language of business, dollars and cents.

In physical appearance, Career Building Letters are most effective when they appear to be personal, hand-typed letters. We suggest using Monarch stationery (7″ x 10″), with a personal embossed logo on top, listing all the relevant information on your personal or business identity, phone numbers and addresses. The letter should be one page, or two pages at most, and pruned of all excessive verbiage.

Optional Paragraphs and Phrases

• If your company needs part-time janitorial help, my firm can bring you twice-weekly service for less than half the average cost of the leading firm in town.

• Your company has enjoyed enviable growth in the last three years. If you're experiencing the same growth pains as similar companies in your field, you're probably needing extra CPA, accounting and computer help to handle your overload. Our firm can help bring your paperload burden under control and prime you for more and greater growth in the future.

- Wouldn't your company find greater unity and strength with a company-wide newsletter? Chances are, you don't have any editorial employees, and can't afford to hire one full-time. My job is to do this kind of work for numerous companies like you, part-time, averaging less than one day a week, for less than the price of printing the letter itself.

- Employee birthdays are special occasions, and we specialize in making them EXTRA special. We have a series of specialized dancers, singing mailgrams, "living birthday cards", and inspirational messages which build employee morale and make lasting memories.

- "The check is in the mail" and "The computer is down" are two of the favorite business half-truths for explaining late payments. We help solve both problems, with a unique financial management system which actually prints and mails checks on-line, for a documented lower price than most manual systems. Let us demonstrate this amazing system for you.

- Two kinds of lawyers are expensive: the ones you hire full-time, and the ones you pay by the hour. There's a middle ground, however: the contract lawyer who works on retainer. He works on specific long-term projects, for a pre-arranged fee, with no expensive "start up" costs, i.e., educating a lawyer in the intricacies of your own business, on your own nickel. This is the kind of service I give to firms like yours.

A.B.C., Incorporated
One Main Street, U.S.A.
(555) 555-5555

Dear   :

    If your company is considering expansion into computer mainframe equipment and software, I may be able to help you.

    You will find that your decision involves far more than hardware and software. It begins with a full-scale evaluation of your business goals and information requirements. I am prepared to launch just such a study for you, from the ground floor up to the programming of the new computer.

    Since 1956 I have worked exclusively in facilities management for every generation of IBM computers. I have been responsible for selecting the software and hardware and then building the teams to run them efficiently.

    In conjunction with major colleges and universities, I have installed and supervised multi-million dollar facilities, and I have also supervised the cost-efficient "lean and mean" operations for small, growing businesses like yours. In each case I can document bottom line savings to my client organization in the six-figure range.

    If you would like to meet to discuss my qualifications for serving your computer needs, I will be glad to consult with you for up to four hours, without fee or obligation, to see if we have a match of needs and goals.

    I will be calling your office next week to see if we can set up a mutually convenient time to explore the potential of computer facilities management at your company.

        Sincerely,

        John Smith

Letter for data processing services

A.B.C., Incorporated
One Main Street, U.S.A.
(555) 555-5555

Dear   :

    If your advertising is not currently working to your satisfaction, consider reviewing my services. The results from my last two direct mail advertising campaigns are outstanding!

    In a major million-piece mailing, my client's immediate profits were over $150,000 which represented a 150 percent return on investment--with promise of much more repeat business from those same customers. The previous mail campaign, with another copywriter, lost 25 percent on the bottom line after three months.

    My most recent sales letter was tested against four similar letters in the mail at the same time to the same lists. Results: mail returns, with $95 checks in them, were 1.24 percent on my letter (for a 186 percent return on the client's investment), while the other three letters returned 1.01 percent, 0.82 percent, and 0.51 percent.

    Profits on both of the above letters, combined, totaled $286,000. My fee was only one-tenth of profits, netting the two clients over $250,000 in new business. If my letters had failed, or just "broken even," I would not have charged a cent to either client.

    Can you afford to be without these kinds of results? After all, it costs you nothing, unless I make money for you. I am willing to spend two hours discussing a direct mail campaign with you, followed by two to three weeks of dedicated work on a two-part mail campaign, all with no risk to you.

    Please give me a call or write to the address listed above if this proposition interests you. We can meet anytime in the next 30 days, at your convenience. After that, my client commitments will keep me busy until next March. Now is the time to take advantage of this narrow window of mutual opportunity.

    Sincerely,

John Smith
John Smith

Letter for direct mail advertising

A.B.C., Incorporated
One Main Street, U.S.A.
(555) 555-5555

Dear   :

    As your office expands, you have probably considered
building an annex or separate wing on your existing building.
Typically, managers will send out bids for construction, then
hire an interior decorator AFTER the construction is finished.
Inevitably, this leads to a far different outcome than you
originally planned.

    At our company we bring a full-service design, construction,
and interior decorating service to you. Our professional staff
can analyze your space needs, design a new building or annex to
best fit those needs, and then supply the construction crew and
interior design consulting.

    With firms your size in this town, we have brought this new
concept of full-service construction to over ten companies. I
have enclosed with this letter three affidavits of customer
satisfaction, and I have many more on file for your inspection.

    The best thing about our service is that the bottom line
cost is lower, and the end results are consistently more
satisfying.

    You may not be in need of more office space at this time,
but my experience is that any company with your growth record
will consider expansion soon. So please give me a call at your
convenience to set up an introductory meeting--either next week
or six months from now--to consider your space needs.

                        Sincerely,

                        John Smith

                        John Smith

Letter for construction and
design services

A.B.C., Incorporated
One Main Street, U.S.A.
(555) 555-5555

Dear   :

    If your company is looking for sales personnel that perform
--and who isn't?--you may be interested in my track record:

    ● With a $10 million-plus manufacturing firm, I was the
leading salesman among a nine-person staff. I accounted for
fully one-third of sales, although I was fourth in seniority with
a decidedly unproductive territory in the beginning.

    ● Inheriting a small and unproductive four-person sales
staff, generating $1.5 million in sales over the previous 12
months, I helped the same basic staff members (with just one
turnover) turn the company around, generating $4.3 million in
sales my first year and $10 million by the third year.

    ● In my first sales work I joined a major insurance firm
and set a branch office record for reaching the "Million Dollar
Club" in my first six months with the firm. After two years I
was the leading salesperson.

    My biggest challenge is turning a company's sales force
around through motivation and strong follow-through techniques.
Now that I have succeeded in building my current staff to top
professional levels at my current place of employment, I am ready
to do the same in a new location.

    If you are interested in a sales manager who can double or
triple your sales within the next 12 to 18 months, please give me
a call to discuss your sales needs.

                Sincerely,

                John Smith

Letter for a sales position

A.B.C., Incorporated
One Main Street, U.S.A.
(555) 555-5555

Dear   :

　　As talk show host on WWXO, I have built the key 3-6 p.m. drive-time slot into the No. 1 rated program in town. When I inherited the position three years ago, we were No. 4 on Arbitron. The additional ad revenues in this time slot alone amount to more than $350,000 per year.

　　I am considering moving to a new market, and I have selected your city as my premier candidate for relocation. After all, I grew up there, and I think I know your people and their needs quite well.

　　The reason I am writing you is to offer the same kind of dynamic radio growth to your market which I have introduced to WWXO. Although there are other stations in your town, I am giving you "first right of refusal," because you are the best station there, in my opinion, although your ratings do not yet reflect the audience you deserve. I take that as a challenge!

　　I will be visiting your city next month and would like to meet you to discuss these matters further. I would like to call you next week to set up a time of mutual convenience. Feel free to call me in the meantime, preferably during the morning hours prior to my afternoon radio work.

　　　　　　　　Sincerely,

　　　　　　　　John Smith

Letter for radio/TV personality

CHAPTER 4

Enhancing Shareholder Relations

No matter what its size, every corporation with shareholders relies on these people both financially and professionally. Shareholders are without a doubt key elements to the success of any business. As a result, a strong, positive relationship must be cultivated and maintained. Since written correspondence is most often how business executives and shareholders communicate, letters are the tools with which a good relationship is built.

For corporations with a number of shareholders (even if the stock is not publicly held), Shareholder Letters are written both to inform and to sell. Shareholder Letters are a good way to ensure investors that their money is invested well. Corporate presidents frequently use shareholder letters to explain any shortcomings in past performance or provide realistically optimistic forecasts of the future. If the firm had extraordinary profits or sales during the past year, you might want to caution the shareholders not to expect that type of growth every year. The letters are an opportunity to emphasize new products and plans. They also serve as a recordkeeping method for the corporate activities and decisions.

Caution: The forms in this chapter are designed exclusively for smaller, non publicly-held corporations. Corporations whose shares are owned by members of the general public are regulated by the Federal Securities Exchange Act of 1934. This Act regulates virtually every aspect of contact between the corporation and its shareholders. The advice of a qualified securities lawyer should be sought before using any of the forms in this chapter.

Shareholder Letters should be personal and informal. You want the shareholder to feel that he is talking directly to the president or chairman. Avoid jargon, even if you think a shareholder of your corporation should be comfortable with it. Use correct grammar and sentence structure, but write in a conversational style.

All letters to shareholders should be accurate. You might want to emphasize some matters and put less emphasis on others. But you cannot ignore unfavorable information or distort its effect. To do so not only risks future legal action but also makes the shareholders wonder what you are hiding. In fact, many business consultants believe that the best way for businesses to handle bad news is to meet it head on and give shareholders a candid explanation of the situation.

A letter to shareholders should say something special. It should not just repeat the numbers from the annual report or other documents that accompany the letter. You should be giving the story behind the numbers and telling the shareholders what they can expect the numbers to look like in the future.

NOTICES OF ANNUAL MEETING

A formal invitation letter is an effective, professional way of notifying your shareholders of an annual meeting.

Tips on How to Customize Your Letters:

1. Open with a cordial invitation to attend or simply a fact listing of where, when, and who.

2. Mention that an agenda is enclosed (and don't forget to enclose one!).

3. Emphasize the importance of attending. You may want to offer the alternative of a proxy. (See the example on page 67 as well as the example of a follow-up to the proxy solicitation on page 69.) Some people would rather have a meeting with a large number of proxies than one with a lot of empty chairs.

Optional Paragraphs and Phrases:

• Under the power given to me by the BY-LAWS of the _____ Corporation, I hereby call the regular annual meeting of the shareholders of the _____ Corporation, to be held on _____ , 19—, at _____ p.m., at the principal office of the Corporation, _____ .

• This annual meeting will be held to elect Directors and transact any other business that may come forth.

• A detailed agenda and list of proposed corporate changes are enclosed.

• Please make every effort to attend this meeting as some very crucial decisions need to be made as to the future of the corporation.

• If you absolutely find it impossible to attend, please fill out the enclosed proxy statement and return it to the above address at your very earliest convenience.

A.B.C., Incorporated
One Main Street, U.S.A.
(555) 555-5555

Dear Shareholder:

The management and Board of Directors of ABC Corporation cordially invite you to attend our annual shareholders' meeting. The meeting will convene at 10 a.m. on Wednesday, March 20, 19 , in the conference room at our corporate headquarters.

The agenda for the meeting is enclosed, and as you can see, there are several issues of interest to all shareholders. Details of these issues are explained in the enclosed proxy statement.

It is important that you make every effort to attend this meeting. If you are unable to attend, please read the proxy statement and return a signed proxy to be voted according to your instructions. Under state law at least 50 percent of the corporate voting stock must be represented at the meeting, either in person or by proxy, in order for any action to be taken at the meeting.

Thank you.

Sincerely,

John Smith

John Smith

A.B.C., Incorporated
One Main Street, U.S.A.
(555) 555-5555

Dear Shareholder:

The annual meeting of the shareholders of the ABC Corporation will be held at 10 a.m. Wednesday, March 20, 19 , at the corporation offices. The shareholders will consider the enclosed agenda and any other business that is properly brought before the shareholders.

If you are unable to attend the meeting, please complete and return the enclosed proxy at least three days before the meeting.

Sincerely,

John Smith

John Smith

A.B.C., Incorporated
One Main Street, U.S.A.
(555) 555-5555

PROXY NO. _____

No. of voting common shares _____

No. of voting preferred shares _____

    This proxy is solicited by the following officers and members of the Board of Directors of ABC Corporation: _____

_____.

    The undersigned shareholder hereby appoints as proxy any one of these individuals to act for the shareholder at the annual or special meeting of the ABC Corporation or any adjournment thereof. The proxy shall have full power of substitution to vote and to otherwise act for the undersigned as fully as the undersigned could vote and act if present at the meeting. This proxy shall expire on _____, 19 .

              Shareholder_____

              Address _____

                      _____

              Signature _____

              Date _____

Proxy for annual meeting

A.B.C., Inc.
One Main Street, USA
(555) 555-5555

Proxy

I hereby appoint Jane Jones ☐, John Smith
☐, or _____
(check one or fill in name of person who will
attend meeting), as my proxy, in my name
and behalf to vote on any matter that may
come before the Annual Meeting of ABC, Inc.
on _____.

Name _____

Company _____

Signature _____

Date _____
(This proxy must be signed by voting members of
ABC, Inc. only.)

Proxy with specific
choices provided

A.B.C., Incorporated
One Main Street, U.S.A.
(555) 555-5555

Dear Shareholder:

This is a reminder to submit the enclosed proxy by March 17,
19 . As you know, our annual meeting will be held on March 20,
and no action can be taken unless there is a quorum at the
meeting. It is not convenient for many of our shareholders to
attend the annual meeting, so we depend on proxies to obtain a
quorum.

Naturally, we would like to see you at the annual meeting in
person. But if you do not expect to attend, please return the
proxy. A duplicate proxy is enclosed with this note in case you
misplaced your original.

Thank you for your attention to this matter and your
interest in ABC Corporation.

Sincerely,

John Smith

John Smith

Follow-up to proxy solicitation

A.B.C., Incorporated
One Main Street, U.S.A.
(555) 555-5555

Dear   :

    We received your signed and dated proxy today and appreciate
your taking the time to complete this small but important task.

    You can be sure that the proxy will be voted in the best
interests of ABC Corporation and its shareholders and that the
officers and employees of ABC will continue working for your
benefit.

                Sincerely,

                John Smith

                John Smith

Acknowledgement of proxy

COVER LETTERS FOR ANNUAL REPORT

The two examples we show give you an excellent choice between a longer, more detailed cover letter and a brief, let-it-speak-for-itself cover letter.

Tips on How to Customize Your Letters:

1. Make your personality clear in the letter. Use your personal stationery.

2. Use informal language and tone.

3. Discuss positives in detail, but don't try to hide any negative happenings. Be honest about them as well.

4. Emphasize specific points of interest so the reader does not overlook them in the detail of the report.

5. Use the letter to summarize the report, your opinion on the company's performance and major changes in the past year that have impacted profitability and future growth.

Optional Paragraphs and Phrases:

• The year-end results for this fiscal year are excellent. Your company has recovered completely from the reversals we experienced in the last two years.

• We should all feel very proud of our accomplishments this year; they are reflected in our bottom line as well as our strong product line and growing customer base.

• We are especially pleased with management's successful efforts to lower expenses and increase productivity.

• The losses of the last two years forced management to tighten its belt to the tightest notch. Needless to say this was painful for everyone concerned, but it has paid off, and for that we are extremely grateful.

• Your board truly believes that the actions taken and the accomplishments made this year will make ABC, Inc. an extremely profitable one for many years to come.

A.B.C., Incorporated
One Main Street, U.S.A.
(555) 555-5555

Dear Shareholder:

We trust you are pleased with the performance of ABC Corporation in 19 . The corporation had significant growth in both sales and net income. Also, it appears that our performance was better than that of most businesses in the industry. By any measure, ABC is a sound and growing company.

While virtually every index of corporate performance points upward, we think the best signal of future growth is our record of sales growth. Other firms in the industry experienced geometric sales growth in four of the past five years. ABC, however, adopted a policy of pursuing only manageable growth. Management was concerned about sales growth outstripping the firm's ability to hire and train qualified personnel and maintain a system of controls to accommodate the growth.

This policy of manageable growth appears to have been successful. This year ABC's sales grew at a comparable rate to past years. Some competitors, however, have had numerous quality control problems, declining sales, and ballooning costs. These firms were forced to cut back while ABC continued on its steady growth path.

Management believes this policy is in the best interests of the shareholders. The stock has seen a steady appreciation in value that has been good for individual shareholders as well as for participants in stock option and profit-sharing plans.

The stock option and profit-sharing plans, in fact, are a major reason for ABC's strong, steady growth. Management believes that outstanding managers and employees should be given an incentive to make long-term commitments to the firm. The incentive plans encourage such commitments and ensure that key employees will act in accordance with the long-term interests of shareholders. Currently, 155 managers hold stock options that were issued in the judgment of the Board of Directors. In addition, approximately 65 percent of our employees participate in a voluntary stock purchase plan and 45 percent have vested interests in the profit-sharing plan.

These incentive plans were carefully structured to ensure that employees and investors have similar goals. The Board believes that these programs are producing the desired results and that employees and investors will continue to prosper together.

The past year has been a good one for ABC. While others in the industry are curbing their growth, ABC plans to continue the growth it has achieved in the past.

For the Board,

John Smith

John Smith

Cover letter for annual
report — detailed

A.B.C., Incorporated
One Main Street, U.S.A.
(555) 555-5555

Dear Shareholder:

The future of ABC Company is very encouraging despite some disappointing numbers in the enclosed annual report. Management has made some strong moves that should produce favorable results fairly quickly.

The past year saw only a slight increase in sales while costs and expenses grew quickly. These trends were identified early in the year, however, and corrective measures were taken quickly. Already we are seeing positive results from the new policies. ABC incurred losses in both the first and second quarters, yet there was only a small cumulative loss for the entire year.

Expenses and overhead were reduced by mid-year, and profit margins were restored quickly. ABC now has a lean and healthy operation. No essential functions or personnel were reduced. Instead, management discovered that some divisions of the corporation had grown far more than was necessary or justifiable. The extra overhead was trimmed, and the firm is now poised for sustained growth.

The Board believes that management reacted quickly and appropriately when problems became apparent. Difficult decisions had to be made, but they were made quickly; and results indicate that the decisions were good ones. ABC has gone through a painful period in its growing process, but we believe that period is over and earnings will return to their past growth rates.

For the Board,

John Smith

John Smith

Cover letter for annual report — general, brief

ACKNOWLEDGING A NEW SHAREHOLDER

Create goodwill, improve your company's public image, and make a sales pitch all with one simple welcome letter to a new shareholder. Always keep in mind that your shareholders may be actual or potential customers.

Tips on How to Customize Your Letter:

1. Give this letter an identity of its own, one that reflects yours.

2. Incorporate your new shareholder into the fold right away by using a lot of "you" and "our."

3. If you feel it is appropriate, tell the new shareholder about your products and company structure.

Optional Paragraphs and Phrases:

- It is a pleasure to welcome you as a shareholder in our company.

- On behalf of the directors and officers of ABC, Inc., I welcome you as the newest member of our shareholder group.

- To help you become acclimated to the company, its standing, and its goals, I've enclosed a copy of our latest annual report.

- You will be receiving all annual and quarterly reports as well as any special notices published. These are the forms of communication through which you will be kept informed of the happenings at ABC. If you have any questions or wish any information outside of these publications, please feel free to ask for them.

- I am confident that you will find this association a mutually beneficial one.

- Please know that we are always anxious for feedback from any of our shareholders.

- Thank you for consenting to become one of our shareholders. We are proud to have you aboard.

A.B.C., Incorporated
One Main Street, U.S.A.
(555) 555-5555

Dear   :

    As president of ABC Corporation, I would like to take this opportunity to welcome you as a new shareholder. I think you have invested your money wisely.

    The purpose of this letter is to assure you that we are indeed partners with the same goal: the long-term growth and profitability of ABC. You will receive our periodic reports describing how well we are achieving that goal, and I hope that you will be able to attend one of our annual meetings so we can meet.

    If you have any questions or comments, don't hesitate to forward them to me. You will get a prompt reply from either me or a member of the shareholder relations staff.

             Sincerely,

             John Smith

             John Smith

Acknowledging a new shareholder

CONTACTING A FORMER SHAREHOLDER

When a shareholder becomes a former shareholder, it is wise to keep up the goodwill and not let him or her float away. This is particularly true if you keep in mind what we said earlier, that a shareholder might very well be a customer.

Tips on How to Customize Your Letter:

1. Express your concern over the shareholder leaving.

2. Ask for a reason why, in a polite, non-pushy manner.

3. Give hope that the reader may one day rejoin the shareholders of your company.

4. Reinforce that thought by offering to continue to send the company's publications and to entertain comments about the company from the former shareholder.

Optional Paragraphs and Phrases:

• We appreciated having you as a shareholder in ABC, and are sorry to see that you have chosen to sell your shares.

• We recently discovered that you are no longer a shareholder in our company. We are sorry about that, especially since your participation in ABC was greatly appreciated.

• If your decision to sell your shares had anything to do with company policy, please let me know right away.

• It will of course be a pleasure to welcome you back as an ABC shareholder at any time in the near future.

• In fact, in order to help ensure that you will be back, we will continue to send all of our company publications and will be happy to hear any comments you may have about the business.

• Thank you again for being one of our shareholders. We hope to see you in that capacity once again very soon.

A.B.C., Incorporated
One Main Street, U.S.A.
(555) 555-5555

Dear   :

    I have been told that you recently sold your holdings in
ABC, Incorporated. As a large and long-term shareholder, your
transfer of shares disturbs me. I believe ABC is one of the best
places to invest money.

    Sometimes stock sales are prompted by factors out of our
control. But other times a shareholder simply loses his
confidence in the firm. If the sale was caused by our recent
performance or our policies were a reason for this transfer, I
wish you would take a few minutes to write me about your
concerns.

    We hope you have profited from our relationship and look
forward to welcoming you back as a shareholder some day.

        Sincerely,

        John Smith

Contacting a former shareholder

SPECIAL LETTER TO SHAREHOLDERS

Occasionally, and let's hope very occasionally, there is a time when bad news needs to be specially communicated to your shareholders. If this situation should happen, be short, sweet and honest.

Tips on How to Customize Your Letter:

1. Explain the situation in the first paragraph.

2. Try to explain briefly what management's position on the decision was and why.

3. If at all possible, state how you think the decision will ultimately be the best for the company and the shareholders.

4. Offer to answer any questions the shareholders may have.

Optional Paragraphs and Phrases:

- ABC has decided to purchase another company.

- As part of the strategic plan we outlined in the most recent annual report, we have been researching acquisitions and have located a good possibility.

- In order to be certain our decision is the right one, we need to hold a meeting of shareholders.

- Since this is a most crucial vote, please do your best to attend the meeting on _____ . If you cannot, please return the enclosed proxy promptly.

A.B.C., Incorporated
One Main Street, U.S.A.
(555) 555-5555

Dear Shareholder:

As you know, ABC's farming operation has not performed well over the last few years and hurt the firm's overall performance. Management has spent much time searching for a solution to this problem and has finally negotiated a sale of the timber operations to Georgia Pacific for $15 million in cash and $20 million in three-year notes.

The management and Board of Directors strongly believe this sale is in the firm's best interests and is on the best terms possible. The sale, however, must be approved by a majority of shareholders before it can be consummated. Therefore, a special meeting has been called for October 25, 19 . The sole purpose of the meeting is to vote on the proposal to sell the timber operation.

We strongly believe that this sale is in the best interests of every shareholder. But this beneficial move cannot be taken unless you attend the meeting or submit the enclosed proxy. The sale is described in detail in the enclosed statement. If you have any questions, please contact our shareholder relations office.

For the Board,

John Smith

John Smith

Special letter to shareholders

CHAPTER 5

Writing to VIPs

Most business executives are active in some combination of activities indirectly related to the success of their careers—be they community, civic, professional, or political. Many of the key contacts made in these associations have made or broken whole business organizations.

Sometimes public participation is forced by circumstances, such as when a state or local government considers a law or tax that could hurt an industry or business in general. Writing politicians and newspapers would then be as important to the business as billing customers.

Community and professional activities normally are a matter of notice. Participants in these activities often find that they first write invitations to speakers, answer such invitations, and accept or decline various positions.

Most of these letters are fairly easy to write. The writer needs only to state all the facts in a direct, concise style. Other letters, such as those to elected officials, require careful writing because the writer must use tact and the right tone. These letters often seek to persuade the reader to a position in which the writer strongly believes.

LETTER TO A LEGISLATOR

It is in every business executive's interest to have as close communication with local and federal legislators as possible. In fact, the success of your business may be determined by the passage of laws in your state capital or in Washington. Let your legislators know what your concerns are, but don't forget to let them know of your support for causes and bills you believe in. It is in the legislators' best interest to pay attention to you; after all, you are a voting citizen and a member of the business community, both of which are greatly influential in the election process.

Tips on How to Customize Your Letter:

1. State your concern and your position clearly in the opening paragraph.

2. Be brief, but clear. If you are referring to a specific bill or proposal, specify the bill number and/or name.

3. Make sure you write the letter so all of your points are heard.

4. Focus on the *public* interest of your concern rather than your personal interest.

Optional Paragraphs and Phrases:

- I understand that the Land Ecology Bill for the state has been temporarily tabled. I don't understand how anything of such vital importance to the outdoor health of this state could be postponed for even a day.

- Thank you for your reply to my letter of _____ . It is a good feeling to know that my thoughts are heard on Capitol Hill.

- I appreciate your shared concern of this matter. You can count on my continued support.

- If there is any way I can help to stop this devastation, please let me know immediately.

- Thank you for your time and attention. Both are greatly appreciated.

- The letter and public statements you recently sent me show that you have given this issue a great deal of thought. Regrettably, I think you have overlooked several significant points.

- We in the industry appreciate your prompt response to our concerns. We're grateful for the hearing you've scheduled and are glad for this opportunity to present our position.

- I don't often get involved in public affairs, but I am threatened by the legislation that is now proposed. There is a great deal of emotional rhetoric being thrown about that obscures most of the facts. I'd like an opportunity to present some of these facts in a face-to-face meeting.

- During your campaign, we were assured that you would take steps to correct this situation. In fact, if the newspapers can be believed, you are working to make things worse. I would like an explanation of this change of position.

A.B.C., Incorporated
One Main Street, U.S.A.
(555) 555-5555

Dear   :

I want you to know how pleased I am with the introduction of
H.R. 2201, the bill requiring used car dealers to issue a six-
month warranty on each used car sold.

As an owner of ABC, Inc., a regional messenger service, I
purchase anywhere from five to ten used cars in a year. The six-
month warranty will greatly save me in repair costs, which can
add up significantly in that amount of time.

Of course, my situation is uniquely more sensitive to the
contents of this bill. However, I firmly believe that the rights
of all consumers are being reinforced by H.R. 2201, an act which
is not only commendable but necessary.

Please let me know if I can do anything to aid in the
passage of this bill and accept my appreciation for your good
work in our House of Representatives.

Sincerely,

John Smith

John Smith

A.B.C., Incorporated
One Main Street, U.S.A.
(555) 555-5555

Dear   :

    I am writing to you about H.R. 2201, a bill that would require used car dealers to issue a six-month warranty on each used car sold.

    This bill is being promoted as pro-consumer legislation, but it would actually have a bad effect on the average consumer. The passing of this bill would result in fewer used cars being available from dealers like myself and higher prices for the cars that are available. Prospective used car buyers will have to buy from private parties through the classified ads. I think this will increase the buyer's chances of getting a "lemon."

    The reason for this is simple, as many car dealers could vouch for. Take my own example for instance. I am a car dealer in your district and have an active used car division in my dealership. Because I value my reputation and respect my customers, I resell only a small percentage of the used cars that come my way. The rest I sell wholesale or sell for parts.

    The cars I resell carry one-month warranties. Each car is worked on from top to bottom before it is offered for sale. In addition, I do whatever is reasonably possible to keep a buyer satisfied; I want him to buy a new car from me someday.

    But used cars not infrequently have hidden defects that even a thorough maintenance check cannot find. I know this, as does any reasonable buyer.

    If H.R. 2201 becomes law, my costs will rise dramatically. I will have to raise the selling prices of my used cars and be even more selective about which cars I sell.

    I have enclosed a brochure on this issue for your consideration. When H.R. 2201 comes up for a vote, I hope you will sharply question those who say this bill benefits consumers.

            Sincerely,

            John Smith

Letter to legislator — concern

LETTER TO A LOCAL OFFICIAL

Your local officials have a hard job. They are employed to work for you, but they rarely know who "you" are. Their jobs would be made much easier and much more effective if you and others wrote to them occasionally to let them know who you are and what concerns you might have.

Tips on How to Customize Your Letter:

1. State your purpose immediately.

2. Proceed to explain your case and why it may affect you in a logical, informative, and concise manner.

3. Emphasize how important the matter is to you in the close.

Optional Paragraphs and Phrases:

• The Wine Institute is more than pleased with the establishment of the Institute for American Wines overseas. We are concerned, however, with exactly how the trade procedures will work.

• Any information you could provide about this situation would help us evaluate our exact position more accurately.

• Since my store is located exactly at the intersection, I more than others would like to see the installation of a traffic light.

• Because of your letter of _____ , we are much relieved about the situation as discussed in our letter of _____ . We are still concerned that the solution may not work in reality. Any assurance you can give us to this effect will be more than helpful.

• Thank you for your prompt attention to this matter. We are proud to have you as one of our public officials.

• I've been following your performance in office quite closely and am impressed. You appear to have not only a genuine concern for the community but also a strong grasp of the issues. This combination is rare, and I hope you will apply it on this issue.

• I want you to know that we are willing to offer whatever aid you need to bring about a successful resolution of this issue. We can provide expert analysis, do research, and compile studies to support the various arguments we are making.

• The life of a public official is very hectic, so I wouldn't write you unless I believed the issue to be important.

• I am something of an expert in these matters and would be glad to appear at any hearings you hold on this matter or supply you with studies or other facts that you might need. This issue is so important that I have already devoted a substantial amount of time to it and will be willing to devote whatever else is needed.

A.B.C., Incorporated
One Main Street, U.S.A.
(555) 555-5555

Dear   :

    I wish to comment on the zoning application of XYZ Company relating to the building at   .

    Our firm has been located on this block for five years. We and the other businesses in the neighborhood have found the neighborhood to be a very friendly and profitable one for small service businesses and restaurants. We do not want to see that atmosphere changed.

    We oppose XYZ Company's zoning application. XYZ wants to convert two of the neighborhood office buildings into multi-family dwellings. The businesses in this neighborhood complement each other very well and thereby contribute to each other's success. The change in use proposed by XYZ would upset this balance.

    In addition, the change would create parking and safety problems. XYZ would provide no parking for the residents. Instead, the new residents would compete for street parking with our clients and customers. With parking already at a premium, this proposed change is untenable.

    We also believe the multi-family dwellings would cause security problems. Presently, police patrols know that the buildings and sidewalks should be empty after working hours. Anyone loitering outside a building can be watched or questioned. If XYZ's buildings become residences, this would change. Police would be unable to determine who belongs on the block and who does not.

    I believe the concerns outlined here are real and significant. I urge you as strongly as I can to reject ABC's zoning application.

                Sincerely,

                John Smith

                John Smith

Letter to a local official

LETTERS INVITING A SPEAKER, COMPLIMENTING A SPEAKER, DECLINING AN INVITATION TO SPEAK, ACCEPTING AN INVITATION TO SPEAK

Inviting someone to speak, complimenting them on their speech, and accepting an invitation to speak are all easy, positive, fun letters to write. Declining an invitation to speak may be a little trickier.

Tips on How to Customize Your Letters:

1. Inviting someone to speak—Compliment the reader on his or her ability, explain in detail the subject of the talk, give all necessary facts as to where, when, why, and who, tell the reader how welcome he or she is.

2. Complimenting a Speaker—Reintroduce yourself, comment on how impressed you were and how you felt the talk benefitted the entire group.

3. Accepting an Invitation to Speak—Express your appreciation, confirm the facts of the event, thank the reader for thinking of you.

4. Declining an Invitation to Speak—Thank the reader for the invitation, give an honest explanation for your having to decline, offer a future possibility.

Optional Paragraphs and Phrases:

FOR INVITATIONS TO SPEAKERS

• I thoroughly agreed with your recent article. These thoughts deserve more exposure, and I wish you would present them in a talk at our monthly meeting.

• You were the only unanimous selection of our speaker's committee, and we are extremely interested in having you address our group. Enclosed is a copy of our meeting schedule for the next six months. Please review it and let me know if any of the dates fits into your schedule.

• Several of our group's members have commented very favorably on the speech you gave at the national convention. Their comments were so laudatory that the rest of us would like you to make the presentation at one of our meetings.

• I know you are busy, so we will be as flexible as possible on the schedule. If you have an alternate date that better suits your schedule, please let me know.

FOR COMPLIMENTING A SPEAKER

• Your speech was one of the best of a season of very good speeches. Several members of the audience said they simply could not say enough complimentary things about the presentation. You really were a hit.

• We really appreciate your taking time to speak to our group. It is rare that we are able to hear a lecture from someone with your expertise and speaking ability.

• Scheduling a speaker often is a hit or miss affair. In your case it was a big hit. We were all very impressed with both your speaking style and the substance of your talk.

• Perhaps the best compliment that can be paid to a speaker is to act on his advice. I can tell you that several members began implementing your ideas within days after your speech.

FOR DECLINING A SPEAKING INVITATION

• Your invitation was extremely gracious. That makes it all the more difficult to conclude that I simply cannot fit another speech into my schedule.

• My schedule has been quite hectic for several years, and I have recently decided to sharply reduce my speaking engagements. Because of that, I won't be able to appear before your group.

• According to my schedule, I won't be in your area near any of the proposed speaking engagements. Therefore, I must decline this invitation.

• I would really enjoy speaking to your group and hope you will offer me another invitation in the future.

FOR ACCEPTING A SPEAKING INVITATION

• I'd really enjoy speaking to your group, and I will be in town for the entire last week of June. I could speak at your scheduled Tuesday meeting at the Shoreham.

• I am happy to accept your invitation to speak at your meeting on March 9 at 7:00 p.m. I will make my own travel arrangements.

• Thank you for your flattering invitation. I am glad to accept it. Since the publication of my article I have conducted some additional research and updated the presentation. I think you'll really enjoy the talk.

• I'm looking forward to speaking to your group and meeting the members.

A.B.C., Incorporated
One Main Street, U.S.A.
(555) 555-5555

Dear   :

   I have recently had the pleasure of reading your articles in
Executive's Report and Time Management. In addition, one of our
association members heard you speak when she was in Boston. We
are both very impressed with your work.

   As program chairman of the local Association of Women
Entrepreneurs, I am inviting you to speak at our August meeting.
We generally meet on the third Wednesday night of each month but
are so favorably impressed with your work that we would be
willing to change our schedule to fit yours. We can offer you
traveling expenses plus a modest honorarium.

   Our usual format includes a cash bar from 6:30 p.m. to
7:00 p.m. followed by dinner until 8:00 p.m. Your speech should
begin shortly after 8:00 p.m. We prefer that your talk be about
30 minutes and be followed by a 20-minute question and answer
period. The audience usually is between 50 and 100 members and
guests.

   If you are interested in speaking before our group and have
some time available in August, please contact me. I know our
audience would appreciate your presentation.

                    Sincerely,

                    Joan Smith

                    Joan Smith

Letter inviting a speaker

A.B.C., Incorporated
One Main Street, U.S.A.
(555) 555-5555

Dear   :

    I cannot tell you how much we appreciated your speech before the Association of Women Entrepreneurs. A number of chapter members have made favorable comments, and booking you has improved my standing in the association.

    Enclosed is a cassette tape of your presentation and a check from the association.

    Your speech was widely appreciated, and we hope to have you speak again in the future.

                Sincerely,

                Joan Smith

                Joan Smith

Letter Complimenting a Speaker

A.B.C., Incorporated
One Main Street, U.S.A.
(555) 555-5555

Dear   :

　　Thank you for your kind words and the invitation to speak at
your August meeting.

　　Unfortunately, I am heavily booked in August and cannot accept another speaking invitation. In fact, my schedule is rather
full through the end of October. I am interested in speaking to
your group if we can work out a mutually agreeable time. If you
come up with some alternate speaking dates, please contact me.

　　Thank you again for your attention, and I look forward to
hearing from you soon.

　　　　　　　　　　　　　Sincerely,

　　　　　　　　　　　　　John Smith

　　　　　　　　　　　　　John Smith

A.B.C., Incorporated
One Main Street, U.S.A.
(555) 555-5555

Dear   :

    I would be glad to speak at the August meeting of the Asso-
ciation of Women Entrepreneurs. The best speaking date for me is
Tuesday, August 16. The only other times I could speak in August
are the 5th and 27th.

    I appreciate your invitation and look forward to hearing
from you soon.

                    Sincerely,

                    John Smith

                    John Smith

Accepting an invitation to speak

LETTER COMPLIMENTING AN ASSOCIATION CHAIRMAN

A letter to the chairperson of a convention, conference, or seminar commenting on a particularly outstanding production will do wonders for establishing important contacts and spreading goodwill.

Tips on How to Customize Your Letter:

1. Be sincere.

2. Be appreciative.

3. Specify elements that were especially outstanding.

Optional Paragraphs and Phrases:

• The conference on Adult Children of Aging Parents held in Passaic, NJ last week was by far the best I have ever attended.

• I have chaired a few conventions in my time, and believe me I know what kind of work goes into them. Yours was fantastic! I never felt more comfortable, nor witnessed such a smoothly run event.

• The industry is still buzzing about the creative and unique arrangements you made for our last convention. Congratulations on a job more than well done!

• Please continue as chairperson for at least one more year. We would like to see you outdo yourself one more time.

• Again, please accept our congratulations. You deserve all the pride that you must be feeling.

• I've been a member of this association for some time, and have seen many chairmen. I have never seen a chairman more dedicated to the job than you.

• A number of members have commented on the quality of this year's program, and I thought you'd like to hear some of these unsolicited testimonials.

• This year the association's activities displayed the high quality that is associated with all your work. We're really lucky to have you as chairman.

• I know this job has taken a great deal of your time, and I regret that you won't be seeking another term as chairman. The organization has a renewed vitality because of your tenure, and I'm sure we will benefit from this experience for some time to come.

A.B.C., Incorporated
One Main Street, U.S.A.
(555) 555-5555

Dear   :

    The annual state convention held last week in Richmond was
the best during my five years in the organization. I can really
appreciate all the time and effort you obviously put into it.

    I think this is the first time that much consideration went
into selecting good speakers for all the sessions and workshops.
Usually the featured after-dinner speakers are the only ones that
receive careful consideration. Your efforts made the entire
weekend a worthwhile experience.

    Congratulations on a quality job, and I hope you will serve
as chairman again in the future.

              Sincerely,

              John Smith

              John Smith

*Letter complimenting an
association chairperson*

DECLINING AN APPOINTED POSITION

Be tactful and sincere, but to-the-point when writing this type of letter.

Tips on How to Customize Your Letter:

1. Make your reason for declining very clear.

2. If you like, ask to be considered for future positions.

3. Thank the reader for considering you and offering you the opportunity.

Optional Paragraphs and Phrases:

• Several years ago I would have jumped at this opportunity, and probably would a few years from now. But at this moment I simply cannot commit the time or attention that I know this job demands.

• My children are reaching a critical age, and I want to spend as much time as possible with them for the next few years. I have spent far too little time with my family recently, and I have promised them that they will receive more of my attention in the future.

• I consider this invitation a very high compliment, and I will be forever grateful for it. But I simply could not do justice to the job if I accepted it at this point in my life. Regrettably, I already have too many other commitments.

• My business requires far too much travel. I enjoy the travel, but it would be impossible for me to be around for key meetings and other events because of my schedule. Perhaps in a few years you will think of me again and I will have a less hectic schedule.

A.B.C., Incorporated
One Main Street, U.S.A.
(555) 555-5555

Dear   :

    Thank you for giving me the opportunity to serve in the
position of Program Committee Chairman of the Association of
Women Entrepreneurs.

    Unfortunately, right now I am already overobligated and
would not be able to do justice to the position if I accepted.

    Please understand how honored I am by your offer and how
much I regret having to decline.

    I hope that when my schedule opens up a bit I will be able
to be involved more fully in your organization.

    Again, please accept my gratitude and apologies.

                Sincerely,

                Joan Smith

                Joan Smith

Declining a position

CHAPTER

6

Creating the Sale

Every letter you write is, in a sense, a sales letter. Even letters rejecting an employment application or a bid from another business should be written in a way that builds good will — or at least does not hurt the business's reputation.

But some letters are written for the sole purpose of generating sales. The direct mail marketing business is one of the growth industries of the decade. Many people expect sellers to come to them, through their mail boxes, instead of having to go out and find deals for themselves. A direct mail marketing campaign is almost essential today for more businesses. Sales letters also can be used to introduce sales representatives or to request appointments for presentation.

A sales letter can be directed to a particular business or individual or can be mailed to a large mailing list. In either case, the writer has the same goals and challenges.

The most difficult part of writing a sales letter is getting the reader started. People generally recognize a sales letter right away and put up a wall of resistance. The strength of this resistance — or the weakness of most sales letters — is evident in the numerous marketing surveys revealing that few sales letters are read past the first paragraph.

The first sentence of a sales letter (or the headline if you use one) is the most important part. The sentence should arouse interest and be concise. Use striking statements, jokes, anecdotes, surprising facts, or unusual offers. Another good ploy is to get the reader personally involved in the letter. Letters can be personally addressed to the reader, or ask him a question, or a favor. But above all, the opening must be original, and benefit-oriented — toward the *reader's* immediate needs, rather than your own.

Once the reader is past the opening, the body of the letter should explain the product or service, and then convince the reader to buy. It is best to keep sentences and paragraphs short and simple. You must convey enthusiasm for the product. In addition, credibility must be established by either summarizing your background, providing testimonials, or offering a free trial or guarantee.

The end of the letter should summarize the entire letter. In addition, the ending should provide a final "hook" to make the reader buy now. The ending should emphasize the bargain you're offering, throw in an additional premium, price reduction, or appeal to one of the reader's needs (ego gratification, financial reward, reduced labor, etc.).

Letters That Sell

There's an old saying: "Sell the sizzle, and not the steak". There's nothing more appetizing than the smell of a sizzling steak, which represents the *anticipation* of delightful consumption. But the same sizzle isn't very tempting once you've eaten the steak. *Anticipation is the better half of realization.* In your sales letter, try to tell the reader what wonderful benefits they will realize, if they respond. But by all means don't give away the "secret" of your product or service. Then, you've robbed the reader of the joys of anticipation.

Every business person, despite their veneer of logic and wisdom, is also a human being, and responds as a feeling human being, with a certain predictable psychological sameness. Everyone has feelings, wants and desires, which your properly written sales letter will acknowledge. Some call these needs the "seven deadly sins", but they're really neither deadly nor sinful. They're the emotions that make us human, and propel us into action. For example, consider....

(1) Pride. The reader's time is valuable, and as he approaches your letter, he wants to know that *you* are aware of how important he is. Do you respect his time, by keeping your letter short, and to the point? Do you recognize that he is part of a special group of carefully selected or "qualified" clients? You better tell him, up front, how important he is, or he might throw your well-reasoned arguments in the trash.

(2) Greed. People want to make money; lots of it. Businesses want profits; that's what drives the engines of the free markets. Your sales letter should show the reader how much money he can make, or save, by using your product or service. Can you double his business, or triple his profits? If you can, that will certainly be an important point to put up front, before he loses interest while reading your detailed proposal.

(3) Fear. Business people fear many things: bankruptcy, bad markets, a severe recession, high interest rates, embezzlement, unfavorable legislation, etc. If you aren't appealing to either pride or greed, then consider fear. Our first sample letter (below) is an example of that: "Read this letter to discover *five hidden dangers* that threaten every business."

(4) Envy. Small businessmen want their businesses to grow. Medium-sized companies want a greater share of the total market. They want to whip the competition in a fair free-market fight. That's envy, a desire to have (legally and ethically, of course) what currently belongs to another. One definition of sales is the "ethical alternative to theft". Recognize this need in your readers by showing them how to increase their market share through your product or service.

(5) Sloth. Remember "The Lazy Man's Way to Riches", a famous long-running ad by Joe Karbo? His "easy way to riches" was to keep promising *other* people an easy way to riches! It constantly made easy money for Joe, because of the universal desire to make money without lifting a finger. A typical way to bring this up in a sales letter is to describe your service as so efficient and cost-effective that it frees the reader's time, on the job, so he can play golf every Wednesday afternoon, or take a trip to the Bahamas.

You get the picture. The reader's needs come first. It would be an error in judgment to think that your product or service is so good that it "sells itself". Sell the *reader*, not the product.

A good sales letter is original. The letters provided in this chapter, therefore, should be used differently from some of the letters in other chapters. The sample sales letters should be read and studied for the qualities that made them effective. You should use these letters to get ideas, not as forms to be copied with small adjustments.

POSITIVE MOTIVATION

The most common and well tested type of sales letter is the one that answers the question "What's in it for me?" clearly and distinctly for the reader. The most obvious letter of this type is the one that says "Have we got a deal for you!!!" Of course, any sales letter to work effectively must be tailored for the product and/or service it is selling. Examples of other sales letters serve as good triggers for ideas, but should be used as just that, not as fill-in-the-blank form letters.

Tips on How to Customize Your Letter:

1. Be sure to state the offer, what the reader will get, up front in either a headline or in the opening sentence. This will be the eye-catcher to entice the reader to move on into the letter.

2. Use a personal tone as often as possible. A lot of "you's" and "your's" help to set the from-me-to-you feeling that has proven so successful over the years.

3. Emphasize the benefits of your product or service over others the reader may have heard of or used.

4. Be extremely clear when describing your offer. The simpler it is, the easier it is for the reader to remember it and make a decision.

5. If you have endorsements from other users, be sure to use them in your letter. There is nothing as reassuring to a reader as hearing from other people who have actually accepted an offer and are satisfied by it.

Optional Paragraphs and Phrases:

• How many times this year have you longed for a new refrigerator, but your budget stops you from buying one? Well, you've longed for your last time this year. Come to our 25th Anniversary Half-Price Sale and get that brand new Fridge for a price your budget can stand.

• Dollar Days Are Here Again!!! Buy one of anything and get another for only $1.-

• Custom Word Processing At Low Prices And Within Any Deadline! We offer 100% accurate word processing services at very competitive prices (we'll beat any bid you may have). We can meet even the tightest deadlines with free pick-up and delivery service. So don't panic in a crunch, just call ABC Typing, Inc.

• Beautiful custom drapery can be yours at ready-made prices.

• We conducted a rigorous survey of consumers and wrote this booklet to respond to the three greatest needs. The booklet explains the new telephone system, how to read a bill, and how to buy phone services at the lowest possible cost. We believe this booklet will not only reduce frustration and confusion but will also cut the average consumer's phone bill by at least 15%.

- This isn't a get-rich-quick scheme. I'm sure you've been burned by such offers at least once before. I have. I'll tell you right now that you will have to take some time to read and study this technique. But I can promise you that you won't be surprised the next time gold or any other investment starts to move. You'll be fully invested and will profit handsomely.

- No doubt you've been offered the secrets of investment success before. You probably responded to one or two of these offers and were disappointed because the "secret" was that you needed a lot of money or technical expertise. That's why I've chosen to tell you the story of an ordinary man who accumulated a large fortune by starting with little money and no great expertise.

- There's much more to running a security service than most people realize—even people in the business. By combining modern management methods with our professional expertise we are able to slash costs while maintaining the security of your facilities. (We can show you around several of our clients' facilities to demonstrate our techniques.) The only one who will notice the difference is the person who writes your checks.

- We're no fly-by-night organization. We've been in this business for 25 years and have won many loyal customers over the years. You can talk to them anytime you want to.

- All the risk of this offer is on us. We won't send a bill until you've had 30 days to evaluate our product. If you're not satisfied, just write us a letter and send it back with the goods—at our expense.

- The difference between a successful investor and an average investor is information. We're in the business of selling investment information. Our time is spent evaluating and interviewing successful investors. When we find a rare investor who has something more going for him than a lucky streak, we learn how he makes his decisions. (Successful investors are more than happy to discuss their methods. All you have to do is ask.) Then we report back to you.

- We have a file full of letters that prove the merits of our product. Here are a few samples:

- Would you like to earn an extra paycheck each year without working one hour more than you do now? I can show you how.

- Investors have lost hundreds of millions of dollars in gold and silver—and it wasn't because they bought at the wrong time. They were taken by obvious frauds.

- I am going to tell you the story of a man who never made over $18,000 a year BUT RETIRED WORTH OVER ONE MILLION DOLLARS.

- Would you like to buy stocks that are worth twice their price? I can show you how.

• A FREE REPORT: 18 WAYS TO SLASH YOUR PHONE BILL. This report is yours with no risk or obligation.

• One year ago I wrote you a letter. I said that you could save $300 a month by choosing our security services. But I was wrong. Our clients report that they've saved an average of $500 per month.

• Do you know which overseas mutual fund appreciates an average of 70% a year and hasn't missed a dividend for 25 years? Do you know that you can invest in this fund, and others like it, for only $1,000?

• I urgently need to inform you of an important and profitable investment situation. Because of the urgent nature of this recent development, I'm mailing this as a first class "Mailgram". Every moment counts. Please take time to read this letter now. Don't delay...

• First of all, be warned.... What you are about to read is so sensitive, so potentially dangerous... so politically explosive, that the entire matter is off limits in the national media. The subject is "untouchable". Here, for the first time in print, is the strange story of how a big brokerage empire started to unravel...

• The Chairman of the Board has asked me to extend to you a rare invitation to join him and an elite group of investors in the most daring, yet potentially most profitable, joint venture you'll hear about this year, and perhaps many years to come. Don't miss out on what could be the AT&T of the 21st Century.

• I'm writing this letter to alert you to a new investment opportunity in real estate, which could double your money over the next three years, and every three years from now on. What's more, every penny is sheltered from taxes.

• If you're over 40, you automatically qualify to receive a free copy of my new $19.95 report, which can make your retirement years rich and rewarding, with a minimum investment of time and money.

• It's an historic profit opportunity, the kind you're likely to see only once every 20 to 30 years. It's almost America's safest and most versatile tax shelter. Finally, it's a rare opportunity to get in at the start of a new cycle—at bargain prices you may never see again. Have you guessed which investment I'm talking about?

• In this letter I will share with you 23 surprising new investment forecasts and recommendations from one of the most respected "prophets" on Wall Street. I'll also show you how to get his $72 Confidential Client Portfolio Recommendations, totally free, without cost or obligation.

A.B.C., Incorporated
One Main Street, U.S.A.
(555) 555-5555

GET A NEW CAR AT HALF PRICE

Dear   :

   You have probably heard of schemes for buying a new car overseas and shipping it to the United States for less than the car's cost on a dealer's lot. Maybe you've heard of "direct factory outlets" that claim to buy cars for wholesale prices as they roll off the assembly line.

   Maybe you know somebody who got burned by actually trying one of these deals. There is a better way.

   Car prices have gone through the roof. Even if you can find a good car at a good price, you still have to finance it. Interest rates today are higher than our parents or grandparents ever imagined they could be.

   There is now a way for you to get a good, reliable car for a reasonable price.

   Previously owned cars can be rehabilitated. Owning an older car does not carry the stigma it used to. Back when cars were reasonably priced, a new car every few years was a sign of success and prosperity. A used car conveyed the opposite image. Today, that's all changed. Most old cars, when properly rehabilitated, are considered classics, status symbols.

   Any car you want can be turned into a brand new machine by our expert mechanics. Give us a car with a good body, and we can turn it into showroom condition for half the cost of today's showroom cars.

   ABC, Incorporated, has been rehabilitating cars for 15 years, long before it became popular to keep a car running for as long as possible.

   You will be happy with our thorough, professional, and guaranteed methods of operation.

   Your car will be completely stripped of old paint and have a new coat of primer with three coats of whatever color paint you desire. The engine and all other working parts will be replaced. The car's interior will be completely redone so that it looks and smells like a new car. An old clunker can be turned into a classic, a symbol of wealth and prestige sitting in your driveway.

Sales letter — positive motivation

A.B.C., Incorporated
One Main Street, U.S.A.
(555) 555-5555

Page 2

It is not surprising that the cost of this work is about half the cost of a new car.

You save the high labor costs and large overhead of car manufacturers. Whenever possible, we take bids and subcontract work to specialists we have worked with for years. You save further on parts bought at wholesale, directly from the manufacturer, not at the inflated prices mechanics and repair shops will charge you for them.

You will not be paying dealer preparation fees and excise taxes. You will not be charged hundreds of dollars for all those little "extras" that are needed to make today's cars presentable.

A rehabilitated car will cost less to operate than a new car. Most older cars do not have costly emission controls and other mandated features. Since you pick the car we rehabilitate, the maintenance costs and gas mileage are largely in your hands.

You do not have to endure the frustration of comparing the costs of your new car to that first car you bought years ago. You do not have to kick yourself for trading in that car just because it had a few thousand miles on it.

You can get that old car back--in showroom condition.

Give us a call, and we will give you a free estimate.

Sincerely,

John Smith

P.S. If you have a particular model in mind and cannot find it, get in touch with us; we can help. Our national network of used car sources can usually find the car you want at a price you can live with.

FEAR MOTIVATION

The sales letter that works is one that is totally original and unique, reflecting truthfully the product and/or service it represents. Basically there are two motivators behind a sales letter: (1) what one will lose if one does not take advantage of the offer, and (2) what one will gain if one does take advantage of the offer. This letter is an example of the first type of motivator — the "fear factor!"

Tips on How to Customize Your Letter:

1. Remember that it is especially important with the sales letters to use the letters provided as *examples* and *idea catalysts* only. The sales letter is not one in which only a few words can be changed for your circumstances.

2. Note the headline. A good way to get the reader interested immediately. Remember to use specifics in all headlines, i.e. "5 Hidden Dangers."

3. With the "fear factor" motivation, be sure to follow up with a proposed solution right away so the reader doesn't get so turned off that he or she stops reading altogether.

4. Prepare your case well initially so by the time the reader gets to your product and/or service he or she will feel that it is utterly necessary.

Optional Paragraphs and Phrases:

• Would you be shocked if I told you that you are probably putting at least one paycheck a year into unnecessary utility bills? Well, 9 out of every 10 people are doing just that. ... But, ABC Energy Management has a way to prevent this.

• What will you do when the IRS seizes your personal assets? Let's hope you never find out. We have a book that will ensure that you never will.

• 1 out of every 5 Americans suffers with headaches without getting adequate relief. This rampant pain is totally unnecessary. Especially now with the new immediate-relief pain deterrent from ABC, Inc.

• So much is changing so fast these days that you need to be an expert on everything, just to keep up with the competition. The biggest barrier to that goal is the muddled information you're getting. It's time you got a weekly 20-minute course in *everything* essential to your business and personal life.... What would that be worth to you?

• How many of the following predictions would have sounded ridiculous if you heard them on January 1, 1987? Yet they all happened, and they were all printed in this newsletter on that day! Just imagine the profits you could have made.... and still can.

- This year, you'll see the return of double-digit inflation, sharply higher interest rates, and, according to my contacts in Washington, an all-out assault by the IRS on your wealth.

- Let me tell you why gold has been acting very mysteriously lately. The answer starts in Zurich, Switzerland, one of the world's leading centers of high finance. On the Bahnhofstrasse — Zurich's "Wall Street" — there's a nondescript building with a placard reading "Wozchod Bank". A Russian bank in Europe? Yes, a Russian bank filled with gold.

- If you're like me, you have probably heard many spectacular success stories of investors who turned something like $25,000 into $500,000, almost overnight. But these stories can be misleading. You see, in most cases, those who have made such tremendous fortunes have two things going for them that you and I don't...

- Remember when gold suddenly shot up to $850—and your money was sitting in a money market fund?

A.B.C., Incorporated
One Main Street, U.S.A.
(555) 555-5555

READ THIS LETTER TO DISCOVER FIVE
HIDDEN DANGERS THAT THREATEN
EVERY BUSINESS--
AND THE STEPS YOU CAN TAKE TO
PROTECT YOUR BUSINESS.

Dear   :

Is your business a candidate for failure? You can find out
by reading the rest of this letter.

Entrepreneurship is on the rise. Most new jobs are created
by new businesses. Business management books are outselling diet
and sex books for the first time in decades. Yet nine of every
ten businesses will fail within five years.

It is relatively easy to pick out the businesses that will
fail. Almost all business failures result from one or more of
the following five causes:

(1) Failure to plan: About 95 percent of new businesses
are started without a written business plan. Yet experienced
managers and consultants believe detailed planning is essential
to long-term business success.

How can you get somewhere unless you know where you are
going, how much it will cost, and which route you are taking?
Adequate planning reduces business failure by identifying many
trouble spots ahead of time so you can solve potential problems
before they become pressing problems.

(2) Lack of capital: Many new businesses make a great
start but find they cannot finish the jobs they started. They
underestimated their needs (a result of inadequate planning) or
ran into higher than expected costs. The founders either close
down the business or sell a large equity interest for a relatively small amount of cash.

(3) No marketing strategy: "Build a better mousetrap, and
the world will beat a path to your door." Unfortunately, the old
saying isn't true. People have to know about your mousetrap, and
they won't find out about it unless you tell them. Many businesses forget this simple fact or believe that word-of-mouth will
make their firms successful.

Worse than no marketing strategy, some firms waste money on
unplanned, uncoordinated advertising campaigns. An unplanned
marketing strategy does not project the right image, reach the
right audience or draw in customers.

(4) Poor personnel planning: The entrepreneur believes in
making it on his own, but he needs some help. He needs to know
when to hire someone, who to hire and what the job description
should be. Personnel decisions such as these aren't very
exciting, but they can make or break a growing business.

(5) Turning over the reins: Most great entrepreneurs are
poor managers. Starting a successful company requires completely

Sales letter — fear motivation

A.B.C., Incorporated
One Main Street, U.S.A.
(555) 555-5555

different skills than managing an established firm. For most entrepreneurs there is a time to step aside or sell the business and move on to another project. Too many entrepreneurs lose their businesses and their fortunes by ignoring this rule.

How do you keep your business from falling into these and other traps?

We Can Help...

ABC, Incorporated, has established a series of products and services to help the small business. We have assisted entrepreneurs for ten years now and have an enviable track record.

We introduce you to our expertise through our book, <u>Small Business Success Manual</u>. This authoritative, easy-to-read book tells you how to spot and solve the problems mentioned above and many others.

You will learn how to improve your cash flow, cut your taxes, and use your business to tap new markets. We have a file of letters, open for inspection, explaining how this book has saved many businesses.

More detailed, personal services are available through our monthly seminars. Our experienced consultants give detailed presentations on every area of successful business management. A brochure describing the seminars is enclosed.

We also offer hands-on consulting to small businesses. Our staff represents decades of business experience, and we guarantee to save your business at least twice our consulting fee on any job we take. If you attend one of our seminars, we give you a free one-hour consultation with the staff member of your choice.

Even if your business is not having problems, there still are ways that you probably are overlooking to make it more profitable. Each of our experts has actual business experience, so we can spot opportunities that escape your attention as you go about the day-to-day routine.

We all live in a volatile economy. The government is constantly throwing surprises at businesses. You cannot do anything about these surprises. That is why you must ensure that predictable business problems are not lurking in the shadows.

ABC, Incorporated, can help. Simply fill out the enclosed order form and join the hundreds of businesses that have benefited from our low-cost products and services. (The form is postpaid. Just put it in the mailbox, and we will get back to you promptly.)

Sincerely,

John Smith

John Smith

Order Form

Yes! Please help me to avoid falling into the traps that await so many business owners.

☐ Send me your free catalogue immediately.
☐ Have a sales representative call me to set up an appointment to discuss the products and services offered by ABC, Inc.

NAME

COMPANY

ADDRESS

CITY   STATE   ZIP

PHONE

NO POSTAGE
NECESSARY
IF MAILED
IN THE
UNITED STATES

BUSINESS REPLY ENVELOPE

FIRST CLASS   PERMIT NO. XXXY   ANYTOWN, USA

POSTAGE WILL BE PAID BY ADDRESSEE

A.B.C., Inc.
One Main Street
USA

LETTER INTRODUCING A SALESPERSON

How a salesperson is introduced to current and prospective clients can set a tone so important it can actually mean the difference between sales and no sales. Customers feel more comfortable with salespeople in the field. Be sure to emphasize both of these points in your letter.

Tips on How to Customize Your Letter:

1. Keep your introductory letter simple, to-the-point, but very businesslike.

2. If a popular salesperson is leaving, be sure to emphasize that he or she fully supports and recommends his or her replacement.

3. Express the new salesperson's background and experience clearly.

4. Let the customer know that the company realizes the importance of top-notch salespeople, which is why John Doe was hired. But, also let Mr. or Ms. Customer know that you welcome any feedback he or she may have about their service, good or bad.

Optional Paragraphs and Phrases:

• We are aware of the excellent working relationship you have had over the past three years with Fred Right. However, we want you to know that although Fred has sought an opportunity elsewhere, before he left he personally trained Gary Left on the proper care of all of his accounts.

• Please let us know, at any time, if there is any change in the quality of your service.

• New things are happening at ABC, Inc. We are expanding our sales staff so our clients can have the personal attention they so richly deserve.

• You have not as yet patronized our business. One reason may have been difficulty in getting waited on. Well, the problem no longer exists. With the appointment of Molly Green, David Small, Kurt Russell, and Delores Ruffsky to our staff we now are proud to boast a complete and very well experienced crew to help with your every need.

• "Doesn't anyone work here?" How many times have you heard or asked that question in a store? Never in ABC Hardware, because of our highly trained and extensive sales staff. In fact, we have just recently hired a new member...

• Although John Franklin has only been with ABC, Inc. for three months now, he has a wide background in sales, especially telemarketing with other organizations, some of which are:

• We are proud to introduce our new regional sales director, Cynthia V. Barrett. Cynthia is a long-time employee who has worked her way up the ladder. There is little about the products in this industry that she doesn't know.

• I'm sending you this note to tell you that I am no longer your sales representative for _____ . I have accepted a better opportunity with the company and am being replaced by George Rutherglen. I've worked with George in the past on several occasions, and I know you will be pleased with him.

A.B.C., Incorporated
One Main Street, U.S.A.
(555) 555-5555

Dear   :

I have the pleasure of announcing the appointment of our new representative in   . James E. Croker, Jr., can answer all of your inquiries concerning computer sales and service.

Jim's strength is business computer systems, and his specialty is word processing. Before taking this assignment, Jim developed his expertise by designing hardware and software programs for more than 150 businesses in the Dallas-Fort Worth area.

We are proud to be associated with Jim and believe you can look forward to better service than ever from our firm.

Sincerely,

John Smith

John Smith

Letter introducing a salesperson

LETTER REQUESTING A SALES INTERVIEW

This letter should be used to show your best side. Customize it to the particular client. Word your request in such a manner that the prospect is almost anxious to sit down with you and discuss what your product and/or service can do for him or her.

Tips on How to Customize Your Letter:

1. Get to the point quickly with this letter in order not to use up too much of the prospect's time. (You want to save that time for the interview itself!)

2. As with most writing, use what are known as ACTION VERBS. For example: "I will demonstrate the equipment on Friday" instead of "The equipment will be demonstrated on Friday."

3. Give a slight indication of the merits of your product and/or service. Be careful, however, not to overdo. If you give your whole pitch in this type of letter, the prospect will yea or nay it before you even have a chance to talk with him or her.

4. Make sure to be very specific in the day, time and location of the requested appointment. You may want to give one alternate day, time, and place to give your prospect some flexibility. If you do give an alternate, be sure to follow up and then confirm the agreed upon facts in writing.

Optional Paragraphs and Phrases:

• You've been a loyal customer for many years, and we thank you. We thought, since you have been satisfied with ABC products in the past, that you might be interested in our latest model and how it works.

• Aren't photocopiers frustrating? I would like to talk to you about eliminating that frustration from your day.

• Will you be available for 30 minutes next week? I hope so, because it might be the most profitable 30 minutes of your year.

• Thank you for taking time to talk to me on the phone this morning. I'd like to confirm our appointment for ...

• I would like to come to your office Thursday, July 18 at 2:30 p.m. to demonstrate our latest coffee maker model. If that is not convenient, perhaps Friday morning at 11:00 would be better.

• Just to confirm our meeting time, you mentioned on the phone that Friday morning at 11:00 (July 19) would be more convenient for you than Thursday afternoon. That sounds fine to me, and I'm looking forward to talking to you about ABC Model Q18 Coffee Maker.

• Would you like to save 10% on every job you do? If you buy ABC electrical supplies, you can.

• We can substantially increase your productivity. Our business computer systems have proven themselves in hundreds of businesses just like yours — even with executives who never touched a computer before.

• I need 30 minutes to tell you how to reduce employee turnover.

A.B.C., Incorporated
One Main Street, U.S.A.
(555) 555-5555

Dear   :

    Do you need a fast, efficient photocopier with low maintenance costs?

    As exclusive regional dealers for   copiers, we can offer you such a copier.

    I have enclosed some literature on these copiers. In addition, I would like you to come to a product demonstration next Friday at lunchtime. Use the enclosed postcard to let me know if you can attend.

    Contact me as soon as possible so you can take advantage of the information right away.

        Sincerely,

        John Smith

        John Smith

Letter requesting a sales interview

POST-INTERVIEW SALES LETTER

One of the most crucial rules of letter writing is to always document your thanks for anything in writing. That holds especially true for interviews. Keep in mind that this includes job interviews, recruiting meetings, staff and sales meetings as well as sales calls. Any situation where you are taking someone's time for a concern of yours is one that merits a follow-up recognition. In a sales call situation, it is especially important, because it will reinforce the professionalism of both the company and the salesperson in the prospect's mind.

Tips on How to Customize Your Letter:

1. First off, thank your prospect for his or her time.

2. Recap your discussion briefly, emphasizing the major selling points clearly.

3. Offer your assistance in answering any questions the prospect may have now or any time in the future.

4. Express in your most straightforward tone that you are very anxious to do business with the prospect and he or she is to let you know how you can help him or her to do so.

Optional Paragraphs and Phrases:

• Thank you so much for the productive and enjoyable meeting of last Thursday.

• It is so nice, Harry, to be able to demonstrate a product, see the appreciation for its efficiency in a client's reaction, and have fun at the same time. Thank you for our visit.

• Enclosed, please find the literature I mentioned at the demonstration on Friday.

• Please tell Mr. Smith I was sorry he couldn't make the demonstration, but I was glad to have the opportunity to make your acquaintance, Dave.

• Since we mostly discussed the actual mechanics of Model X14 on Wednesday, I would like to follow up with some more important benefits it can provide your organization.

• Again, it was a pleasure meeting with you on Monday. I look forward to doing business with you in the very near future.

- Remember, Diane, if you have any questions, concerns or comments, please let me know. Consider me your personal representative for the ABC Corporation.

- Please consider how we can work together on the project you mentioned. Maybe another meeting would be beneficial to you?

- It was a pleasure meeting with you last week. I appreciate the time you took to listen to my presentation on Monday. I'm sure you learned enough to make it worth your while.

- A business computer system is a complicated purchasing problem. Since we talked last week, I have thought of several additional factors for you to consider.

- My job is to do whatever I can to keep you happy with our products. If there is anything that you need, including additional discounts, just give me a call.

A.B.C., Incorporated
One Main Street, U.S.A.
(555) 555-5555

Dear   :

    I really enjoyed meeting with you yesterday. We have a lot
to offer each other, and I am very impressed with the way your
business is run.

    I believe our firm will be able to participate in the
Needham project along the terms we discussed yesterday. As soon
as your firm determines what its role should be, call me so we
can get together and iron out the details.

    I look forward to hearing from you.

        Sincerely,

        John Smith

        John Smith

Post-meeting sales letter

A.B.C., Incorporated
One Main Street, U.S.A.
(555) 555-5555

Dear   :

    I enjoyed demonstrating our line of copiers to you
yesterday. I gather that our copiers can solve many of the
problems you have experienced with other brands.

    Enclosed are the figures I promised you. No doubt you will
see that we can offer a substantially better deal than you are
getting now.

    Call me if you have any more questions. I look forward to
hearing from you again.

                 Sincerely,

                 John Smith

Post-demonstration sales letter

CHAPTER

7

Turning Inquiries Into Sales

Inquiries about products or services are a gold mine that many businesses overlook. Every business should have on hand standard letters that help turn inquiries into sales and long-term business relationships. These letters, written with great care, can be a prime part of your marketing strategy.

In addition to being prompt, a good response to an inquiry includes the following elements:

- An acknowledgement of and expression of thanks for the inquiry
- Detailed responses to questions in the inquiry
- Enclosures providing additional information
- An offer to answer further inquiries or give other assistance

A response to an inquiry is an opportunity to tell the potential customer about many of a business's goods and services, not just the ones mentioned in the inquiry. But the business faces two problems with exploiting this opportunity. First, the response letter must be written so that the reader is enticed into examining the enclosures. Second, you should be careful not to enclose too much additional material with the letter.

The sample letters that follow can help with the first problem. Business judgment is needed to solve the second.

The following pages include several complete letters and additional samples of the different parts of a good response letter.

GENERAL RESPONSE TO AN INQUIRY

Inquiries can be generated by a number of different means. They can come from sales letters, word-of-mouth, or actual mailings soliciting inquiries alone instead of a sale. In any case, they must be answered as quickly and as effectively as possible, because they are actually a giant first step toward closing a sale. The prospect is interested. Now what you have to do with your response letter is turn that prospect into a buyer.

Tips on How to Customize Your Letters:

1. Open your letter with a specific answer to the inquiry. Include mention of the product or service, or an exact list of enclosures if you are sending information with the letter.

2. Then assure the prospect of the quality of the product and or service to reinforce to him or her that the right move was taken when the inquiry was made.

3. Stress sales points that will make the difference between the prospect buying the product or service and just saying "Hmmm, that's interesting" as they throw your letter away.

4. Mention things that set you apart from the competition: your reputation, your service techniques, the quality of your merchandise, and any discounts you can make available to the prospect.

5. If there is any part of the inquiry your company cannot fulfill, be sure to enclose a referral to a company who can give the prospect what he or she is looking for. This will make you memorable.

6. Finally, close on as personal a note as possible. Make the reader feel answered.

Optional Paragraphs and Phrases:

• Thank you for your interest in our seminar program. Under separate cover, I am sending you a copy of "How to Start and Survive in Your Own Business," and a brochure with our full price structure.

• John David, our Vice President of ABC Cleaners, is the person who can answer your questions fully. He, unfortunately, is on vacation this week. I have, however, left a message with his secretary to have him respond to your inquiry as soon as he returns. In the meantime, I've enclosed a brochure on Industrial Strength Bright-N-Easy and a catalogue of our products for your information.

- Thank you for taking the time to ask about our services. If I can be of any assistance in providing those or other services, please let me know right away.

- The enclosed brochure gives you a complete picture of our company, including our production facilities, copies of our latest financial statements, and a brief history of the firm.

- We are pleased to learn from your recent inquiry that you are interested in

  _____ .

- The information you requested is on its way to you.

- Your interest in ABC, Inc. is gratifying. We are sending under separate cover the information you requested. In addition, we have enclosed information about our company that we send to all prospective customers.

- Thank you for your interest in our products. Information on the particular product you requested _____ (name product) is enclosed.

- The enclosed brochure contains the information you requested in your letter of August 9. Please refer to page _____ .

- The enclosed booklet describes the product you asked about. The booklet answers the most frequently asked questions. All the fascinating aspects of the product, however, could not possibly be fit into this small publication. If you have any questions that are not answered in the booklet, feel free to call or write us for additional information. We will reply promptly.

A.B.C., Incorporated
One Main Street, U.S.A.
(555) 555-5555

Dear   :

    Thank you for your interest in our products. We are glad to enclose our catalogue and price list.

    For over   years, our products have satisfied thousands of customers in the   industry. Our experience, technological know-how and advanced production facilities enable us to offer quality products at the most competitive prices in the industry. We believe that after examining the enclosed information you will choose to join the ranks of our satisfied customers.

    Please let me know if I can provide further information or assistance. You can call collect or use our toll-free number.

                  Sincerely,

                  John Smith

                  John Smith

General response to an inquiry

AGGRESSIVE RESPONSE LETTERS

The preceding letter was one which basically responded to a propect's questions. It had some sales effort incorporated, but mainly appeared to be a general response. There is a letter you can write which is a sales letter through and through, while also responding to a prospect's inquiry. We call this type of letter an "Aggressive Response." No doubt is left in anyone's mind that the person who writes this type of letter wants to make a sale. And, oftentimes, as we all know, the direct approach is the most successful.

Tips on How to Customize Your Letters:

1. Formulate your opening as though it was a welcome to the company ("We are glad you are thinking of purchasing an ABC computer." or "We are proud to have you join our family of conference attendees.")

2. Sort of skim over the answer to the inquiry, i.e. "After you have read the information enclosed, you will see that our selection of vacuum cleaners is as extensive as they come."

3. Then concentrate on your sales pitch. Basically, insert all the elements of a sales letter here.

4. You may want to anticipate price questions, and insert a price list or at least the prices of the items the reader inquired about.

5. Close this type of letter with the same personal offer of further assistance as a general response to an inquiry. You may, however, want to add a specific follow-up device such as a time you plan to call the prospect, or some times you are available for a demonstration meeting, etc.

Optional Paragraphs and Phrases:

● I noticed from your return address that one of our sales branches is located approximately ten minutes from you. If it is convenient for you, I would be more than happy to arrange a demonstration of our computer equipment. Next Thursday at 3:00 p.m. is good for me. Please let me know if that is a good time for you. If not, we can arrange a meeting at your convenience.

● Thank you for your interest in ABC Publishing. I can see from your letter that you are familiar with some of our other products, so you know the quality of our product and service. I have enclosed a brochure on the Small Business Wealth Builder, our newest publication. After you have looked it over, the following benefits to you, the small business owner, will probably be evident:

● Your interest in ABC Computers' latest software line allows me to direct you toward the smartest business decision you will make this year.

● From the description of your needs in your letter of _____ , I am happy to say that our Model 546 will comply exactly with your situation.

- To let you know that what I've said is valid and tested, I've enclosed a few comments from our present users. As you can see, some of the largest corporations in the country are very satisfied customers.

- I would like to hear more about your organization so I can offer you some customized advice. Please call me at XXX-XXX-XXXX to set up a meeting appointment at your earliest convenience.

- Certainly you will agree that here is a great investment for every small business owner. No longer will entrepreneurs need to pay large legal fees in order to maximize the tax benefits the law allows.

- Thank you for requesting our free booklet, *22 Ways To Slash Your Energy Bills*. We proudly enclose this useful publication. Before turning to the booklet, however, let me tell you a little about our company.

- Thank you very much for your letter of February 4 and the description of your needs. We have drawn up the enclosed proposal and believe it fully meets your requirements. If you have any questions or feel the proposal is not satisfactory, please let us know.

- One of our manufacturer's representatives is near you. I have enclosed his business card and am forwarding a copy of this letter to him. I am sure that he will be in touch with you soon and can answer all of your questions.

- Turn right now to the enclosed booklet. Open it to page 17. Here are pictured the five best-selling models of our _____. The photographs show the beauty and quality of our products. The descriptions under each picture help you discover which model is right for you.

A.B.C., Incorporated
One Main Street, U.S.A.
(555) 555-5555

Dear   :

    It is a pleasure to send you the information you requested, and we are glad that you are thinking of our company in connection with your computer needs.

    As you examine the enclosed material, you will see that each piece of computer hardware and peripheral equipment fits neatly into a flexible, comprehensive system. In addition, you will note that each item is designed with quality, attractiveness and ease of operation in mind and is complemented by a complete range of software.

          offers the most complete and versatile systems available for the small business. When matched with the vast amount of software available, there is no small business task our systems cannot handle. Whether you need help with payroll, budgeting or word processing,   CAN HANDLE IT.   Do you maintain a mailing list of customers? Is your billing system too slow?   systems and software can solve your problems.

          computers received favorable reviews in leading computer publications. Our firm has manufactured electrical components for over 20 years and enjoys an enviable reputation for quality, innovation and service.

    We hope that you will soon join the growing list of satisfied   customers. We can give you a list of businesses in this area that are using our products to make their operations more efficient and profitable.

    If you need any more information or assistance, please let us know.

                Sincerely,

                John Smith
                John Smith

Aggressive response letter

A.B.C., Incorporated
One Main Street, U.S.A.
(555) 555-5555

Dear   :

    Thank you for your interest in ABC, Incorporated. Enclosed
is the latest issue of our monthly Small Business Wealth Builder.

    The Small Business Wealth Builder is designed to help those
individuals who took the smartest step anyone can take--going out
on their own. This low-cost monthly newsletter is written by
experts in clear, easy-to-understand language and allows you to
immediately start reaping the benefits of hundreds of laws, loopholes, subsidies, tax breaks, investment credits and borrowing
opportunities open to the small business owner.

    Readers of our publication learn hundreds of proven ways to
use their businesses to--

*Make a killing in real estate

*Buy other businesses without putting up a cent of their own
 money

*Get all the cash they need from tax shelter deals

*Divert $5,000 a year or more from their businesses to their
 own use--and not pay a cent of tax on it.

    If you make just one correct business decision based on the
advice you receive in Small Business Wealth Builder, you will
have paid for the cost of a subscription hundreds of times over.

    A response card describing our no-risk introductory offer is
enclosed. Just fill out the card and mail it in the postage-paid
envelope to start receiving this valuable publication today.

            Sincerely,

            John Smith

            John Smith

*Aggressive response letter
with response device*

Small Business Wealth Builder

Four Issues FREE Plus the $29.95 Manual—FREE!

☐ **Yes,** please send a full year—12 information-packed issues—of **Small Business Wealth Builder** at the special Introductory Trial Rate of $48—a savings of $12 over what others pay for a regular subscription. Put another way, this is the equivalent of receiving the first four issues Free. Also send the 120-page manual, **Guaranteed Wealth Building Strategies For Small Business**—a $29.95 retail value—as my Free Bonus Gift. If dissatisfied in any way, I may cancel in the first three months and receive a prompt and full refund—my entire subscription price will be returned to me—and I may keep the issues and the manual Free, with no further obligation.

☐ One Year (12 issues) $48 (Save $12 off regular rate)

☐ Two Years (24 issues) $96 (Save $24 off regular rate)

☐ Payment enclosed

Charge my ☐ MasterCard ☐ VISA ☐ American Express

_____
ACCT NO.

_____
EXP. DATE

_____
SIGNATURE (Required for Credit Card Orders)

Please make any corrections in your name and address. Thank you.

© A.B.C., Incorporated MCMLXXXV

Small Business Wealth Builder

NO-RISK GUARANTEE

You must take an additional $1000 tax-free cash out of your business...or save $1000 on your personal income tax within 3 months, or you will receive a prompt and full refund—every penny you paid will be returned to you No Questions Asked.

Mail Today!

NEGATIVE RESPONSES TO AN INQUIRY

As we mentioned earlier, a response to an inquiry is really a different form of the sales letter. However, when you can't respond in a manner that will completely satisfy the inquirer, your job becomes a little more difficult. The solution is tact. Be gentle and polite when you tell your reader that the information or answer he or she seeks is unavailable. Then offer some sort of alternative. The alternative is where you can still fit in your sales pitch, to whatever degree you feel is appropriate.

Tips on How to Customize Your Letters:

1. Always, always, always use tact!

2. State the reason for your inability to answer the inquiry clearly and right away.

3. Offer straightforward and feasible alternatives. Be specific. Go so far as to enclose other, similar information for the reader explaining that their original request will be honored as soon as possible.

4. Thank the reader for his or her interest and, in this case, patience.

Optional Paragraphs and Phrases:

• Thank you for your interest in ABC Software #43. This particular package has been replaced with a more current and user-friendly Software Package #45. I am taking the liberty to enclose our literature on #45 for your information.

• I realize the literature I've enclosed is not exactly what you were expecting. I do think, however, that after you have looked through it you will see that the benefits of this model are as many or even more than the model which is no longer in production.

• Again, I am sorry we couldn't be of more assistance. Please let me know if there is any other way I can be of help to you.

• There will be a slight delay in getting the information you requested to you. The popularity of ABC Industrial Strength Cleanser has spread so fast we've run out of catalogues. The new ones are on the presses right now, and we should have yours to you within two weeks.

• Thank you so much for your patience. We hope this delay will not be too much of an inconvenience to you.

• We are sorry to say that the Paint Division of ABC, Inc. has closed it doors. You may want to contact the following paint distributors, all of whom come highly recommended.

- Thank you for your letter of _____ . Unfortunately, it seems as though you have ABC, Inc. confused with ABC Industries. We, ABC Industries, produce various types of industrial cleansers and equipment. ABC, Inc., on the other hand, is a business consulting firm. Allow me to give you their address: _____ .

Sorry about the mixup. If you ever need anything in the way of industrial cleansers or equipment, please don't hesitate to give me a call. My extension is XXXX.

- First, I must apologize for the delay in our response. The address of ABC, Inc. has been changed, and since you sent your letter to our old address, I just received it yesterday.

- As a result of time passing due to your letter getting lost in the postal system, our fall special on industrial rags has ended. We will still be happy to offer the discount to you. I've enclosed a specially marked catalogue for your convenience.

- I am very sorry we cannot assist you any longer in the area of paints. Please let me know if you are interested in any other of our products and services.

A.B.C., Incorporated
One Main Street, U.S.A.
(555) 555-5555

Dear   :

We appreciate your recent letter inquiring about our line of tax-saving publications.

Unfortunately, all these books are out of date because of recent changes in the tax laws. The publications currently are being revised. We feel it would be a disservice to sell the current inventory of obsolete books, though this has been a very expensive decision for us.

Your name is being retained, and we will send you a notice about the new editions of the tax books as they are published.

Thank you for your interest.

Sincerely,

John Smith

John Smith

A.B.C., Incorporated
One Main Street, U.S.A.
(555) 555-5555

Dear   :

    We were pleased with your recent request for information
concerning our mutual fund timing services.

    Unfortunately, we cannot comply with the request because we
sell the service only through registered investment advisors. A
great deal of explanation and discussion is required before a
client and his advisor can decide which timing service is appropriate for him, and we prefer to have a client's own advisor
conduct these discussions.

    In case you do not have an advisor, I have enclosed a list
of advisors in your area who have worked with us in the past. We
are not recommending or endorsing any particular advisor or group
of advisors. The list is solely for your convenience.

    Thank you for your interest, and I hope we will have you
join our growing list of clients.

                                Sincerely,

                                John Smith

                                John Smith

Negative response to an inquiry —
alternative response

A.B.C., Incorporated
One Main Street, U.S.A.
(555) 555-5555

Dear   :

Thank you for your recent inquiry regarding tax preparation services.

Regrettably, you seem to have our firm confused with another. We are a financial planning organization. We do provide some advice on tax planning and tax shelters, but we do not engage in tax return preparation.

For your information, I have enclosed a brochure that further describes our services.

Thank you again for your inquiry, and I hope we will be able to help you in the future.

Sincerely,

John Smith

John Smith

Negative response to an inquiry —
wrong company

CHAPTER
8

Following Up
the Sales Pitch

Not every customer will decide whether or not to buy from you after the initial sales letter or presentation. Often one or more follow-up letters are necessary to make a sale, particularly for businesses selling high-priced products. Good sales campaigns sometimes involve sending a series of letters to potential customers.

Follow-up letters can also be sent to established customers. Someone who responded favorably to a prior sales campaign is a good prospect for sales of other items or additional sales of the same item. A follow-up letter can win back old customers or remind present customers of your continuing willingness to serve them.

The difficulty in writing a follow-up letter is that the writer must establish the continuity between the sales presentation and the follow-up letter, yet it must be clear to the reader that new facts or arguments are being presented. If the follow-up letter appears to be nothing more than a repetition of prior sales pitches, the letter will not be read.

A follow-up sales letter should come to the point quickly. In addition, the letter must contain new points or a new offer. The new items should be prominently stated early in the text. If prior arguments are also summarized in the follow-up letter they should be presented in a different order or a new format should be used.

Effective New Elements for a Follow-up Sales Letter Include:

- a special discount, particularly due to an oversupply or limited to a small number of customers
- new literature presenting additional points
- thanks for past orders or expressions of interest, and
- highlighting the ease of ordering from you.

ASKING FOR CUSTOMER'S HELP

There are many approaches to following up a sales call, sales visit, sales letter, or sales interview. The most effective is in the form of written communication. But, even in the area of the of follow-up *letter* there is quite a variety in styles. This letter uses the approach of asking the already-contracted customer for help in analyzing the reaction to a proposal. It gently reminds the customer to react to a proposal, even if it was not accepted favorably. The salesperson writing this type of letter is accomplishing two things: (1) a response to a proposal, and (2) a study of the reaction to the proposal, whether good or bad, which will aid in subsequent sales calls and proposals.

Tips on How to Customize Your Letter:

1. Start the letter off with a semi-personal tone. Give a familiar impression to the reader.

2. It might be a good idea to reintroduce yourself right at the beginning of the letter. (For example, "As your account representative, I want to ask for your opinion on the proposal our company, ABC, Inc., submitted to you last month.")

3. Adopt a slightly, but not overly apologetic, tone. You want to make sure that the reader isn't bothered by your follow-up, but you also want to get a response from him or her.

4. Close the letter on another offer to help the reader, aid him or her in anyway, in other words, keep your selling opportunities open.

Optional Paragraphs and Phrases:

• As your account representative, I want to ask for your opinion on the proposal our company, ABC, Inc., submitted to you last month.

• I would like to take just a minute of your time to ask you a question that may prompt you to make a cost-effective decision.

• Your schedule is a busy one, I know. I thought a letter may be more convenient for you to answer than a phone call.

• You've had an opportunity to become familiar with our _____ . We want to know your opinion of it.

- Did you receive my letter describing our security system? We sent it a month ago.

- If you will notice in my proposal of _____ , I am offering you an additional six months to your subscription—free of charge. Is this something you can use or would a personalized 3-ring binder be more to your liking?

- If you are not interested in our proposal, we would still appreciate a brief explanation as to why not. This would help us to meet your needs more accurately next time.

- Please fill out the enclosed questionnaire and return it to me in the postage-paid envelope provided for your convenience.

- Thank you in advance for taking the time to help us provide the most personalized service available.

- I know how valuable your time is, but hopefully the information you offer will allow us to present immediately acceptable proposals in the future.

A.B.C., Incorporated
One Main Street, U.S.A.
(555) 555-5555

Dear   :

     A letter is less of an interruption than a phone call, so I
am using this letter to ask you to do me (and perhaps yourself,
too) a favor.

     Will you review the proposal I sent you last month and give
me your frank opinion of it?

     We do not want to bother you if you are not interested, but
an evaluation of our proposal and how we might fit into your
plans would be greatly appreciated.

                                   Sincerely,

                                   John Smith

                                   John Smith

Sales letter follow-up — asking
for customer's help

HAS LETTER BEEN RECEIVED?

Nothing is as frustrating as making a sales call, or writing a sales letter and getting no response whatsoever. The prospect is more than likely not maliciously trying to drive you crazy. He or she probably has forgotten your letter or call or has put it under the infamous pile of "things to do when I get a chance." A friendly, slightly humorous, gentle reminder is exactly what is called for here.

Tips on How to Customize Your Letter:

1. Give the reader an excuse right up front by suggesting that they may not have received your letter.

2. Give specific questions you want the reader to answer.

3. Make your role as a provider of service clear.

4. Make the response procedure as convenient for your reader as possible.

Optional Paragraphs and Phrases:

• I wonder if my letter of _____ got lost in the mail.

• Our correspondence may be crossing in the mail. I hope not, because I would like to ask you a few questions without taking much of your time.

• I realize you have many pressing concerns right now, but I would appreciate just a few more minutes of your time.

• Please let me know if there is anything I can add to our proposal of _____ _____to make it more clear and appealing to you.

• Thank you so much for your time. I hope we can begin further discussions on our proposal very soon.

• You can answer a question that is baffling us.

A.B.C., Incorporated
One Main Street, U.S.A.
(555) 555-5555

Dear   :

    I NEED A FAVOR FROM YOU.

    Could you tell me whether or not you received my letter last month? If you read the letter:

    *Did it answer your questions?

    *Are you still interested in our firm?

    *Are you still looking at other plans?

    If you have any problems or questions that were not addressed in our previous letter, please let us know. I have enclosed a postage-paid, pre-addressed reply envelope for your convenience, and you can write your response on the back of this letter. Would you please let us know where we stand?

        Sincerely,

        John Smith

        John Smith

Sales letter follow-up — has letter been received?

SEVERELY DELINQUENT DELAY

Every so often there's a sales effort made that has no response even after several months. Mostly, these efforts are filed under "W" for "Waste of Time." Wrong attitude. It's worth one more try. The prospect may very well have misplaced your literature or have been too busy to respond. A friendly reminder with an added incentive just might close the sale for you.

Tips on How to Customize Your Letter:

1. Take on a business-like tone from the beginning.

2. Make the point early on that the reader has not responded to your offer.

3. Then go immediately to the favor you will do for the reader now.

4. Be sure to re-explain your original offer.

5. Close the letter with an easy way for the reader to respond and a clear understanding that the ball is in his or her court.

Optional Paragraphs and Phrases:

• We've given you a few months to consider our offer but still haven't heard anything.

• I'm not sure if you've been too busy to respond, or you weren't satisfied with our first offer. Either way, I've decided to make the offer even more enticing and give you another chance to respond.

• The main point is, that we want to start an ongoing business relationship with you.

• I haven't forgotten my original offer, but in 3 months you might have. Let me present it one more time, incorporating the new bonus I just mentioned.

• Please use the enclosed form to accept our offer or explain why you cannot do so at this time. A postage-paid envelope is also enclosed for your convenience.

• This morning my assistant handed me your inquiry from last March and said we hadn't heard from you yet.

• I was reminded this morning that we haven't heard from you since your inquiry of two months ago.

• Three months ago you expressed an interest in our service. I'd like to give you an update on what is available.

A.B.C., Incorporated
One Main Street, U.S.A.
(555) 555-5555

Dear   :

    I was looking through our records recently and noticed that
you have not responded to the offer we sent you a few months ago.

    We thought we made a good offer, but obviously it was not
good enough. So we are going to make it even better. If you buy
a year's worth of our service within the next 30 days, we will
add <u>one month of free service</u>. We want you as a customer, and
this offer shows how serious we are. This bonus is in addition
to everything in our previous offer.

    Several months is a long time to remember a letter, so I
will review our offer...[state the facts of your offer here]

    It is your move now. I have enclosed an order form and
postage-paid envelope for your convenience. If this offer still
is not enough, please use the envelope and the back of the order
form to tell me how this offer could serve you better.

    I look forward to hearing from you soon.

                Sincerely,

                John Smith

                John Smith

Sales letter follow-up — severely
delinquent delay

DATE _____

CLIENT NAME _____

COMPANY _____

ADDRESS _____

CITY _____ STATE _____ ZIP _____

PHONE _____

□ **Yes, we would like to take advantage of your offer as outlined below as well as the free month's worth of service offered in your letter of** _____.

Specifics of Offer
_____

□ **Check is enclosed**

□ **Charge my:** □ **MasterCard** □ **VISA** □ **AMEX**
_____

□ **I need more time to consider your offer. Please contact me again on** _____.

□ **No, I am not interested. See reverse side for reasons.**

REMINDER

A good, standard procedure to make a habit of is the two-week after reminder notice. If a brief, polite reminder note is sent to the reader approximately two weeks after a proposal or offer is made it may prevent the very common no response or 2 to 3 month delay.

Tips on How to Customize Your Letter:

1. Keep it brief!

2. State your purpose and the exact time span in the first sentence.

3. Let the reader know candidly that you are reminding him or her of something. Don't beat around the bush!

4. Offer the reader an out by suggesting that he or she may have accepted someone else's offer. Then ask why.

5. As with any sales correspondence, make it as easy as possible for the reader to respond by enclosing a post-paid, addressed envelope.

Optional Paragraphs and Phrases:

• We made an offer to you on _____ , and haven't heard anything from you.

• Since it has been two weeks since we sent our proposal, I thought I would remind you quickly of the timeliness of this arrangement.

• The proposal I sent is a good one, but if you are having second thoughts or have any questions, please let me know.

• A postage-paid envelope is enclosed. I hope to hear from you one way or the other soon.

• If calling is more convenient for you, please feel free. My extensions are XXX-XXX-XXXX and XXX-XXX-XXXX.

• Because of your obvious interest in the product, I am enclosing a brochure about our _____ .

A.B.C., Incorporated
One Main Street, U.S.A.
(555) 555-5555

Dear   :

    Two weeks ago we sent you a proposal for   .

    We have not heard from you, so we thought you would appreciate this reminder to review the proposal. We would like to do business with you and believe our proposal is a good one.

    If you chose another proposal, could you please let us know? Any comments you have would be appreciated.

    A stamped, pre-addressed envelope is enclosed.

    Thank you for your consideration.

                Sincerely,

                John Smith

                John Smith

Sales letter follow-up — reminder

"HURRY—THE SALE'S GOING TO END"

There is a type of follow-up that is less of a follow-up and more of a planned second step sales technique. You send one letter explaining a sale and then in a calculated period of time you send another. This second letter should be written to gently, but firmly, press the consumer's panic button to buy your offer.

Tips on How to Customize Your Letter:

1. Put all of your specifics: date, offer, how much time left, in the first paragraph.

2. Start the letter off with a slight tone of urgency (i.e., I hope you haven't missed it already, but ...).

3. Express your reminder as a favor to the reader and the sale or special offer as a sacrifice to you.

4. Offer a challenge, (i.e., check around for a better price...).

5. Close by setting a date for a second and final "reminder."

Optional Paragraphs and Phrases:

• I hope the mail doesn't prevent you from taking advantage of our special offer.

• There are only five work days left for you to take us up on the incredible offer we made you 10 days ago.

• The absolute last day for this offer is _____ . I can make no exceptions, which is why I'm writing to urge you not to put off your decision any longer.

• If our offer sounds too good to be true, it's because it is! Look around at our competitors, you'll find lower prices nowhere. I guarantee it!

• Seriously, I don't know when or even if we will ever be in a position to make an offer like this again. Please take us up on it.

• I'll be phoning you personally Thursday morning to make some last minute arrangements.

• I have some information that is very important to you.

• Are you aware that you still can get a free 30-day trial of our service?

• You might want to know that over 300 people have subscribed to our service since I last wrote you.

A.B.C., Incorporated
One Main Street, U.S.A.
(555) 555-5555

Dear   :

I sincerely hope this letter reaches you in time. As I told you in my previous letter, mailed ten days ago, we have a special year-end inventory sale ending February 28. That is only four days away.

Since we cannot possibly extend this sale beyond February 28 (for tax purposes), I am writing this urgent letter to remind you that there are only four days left to "take advantage of us." We are actually taking a loss on each piece of equipment--I will show you my factory invoices if you do not believe me--so the only possible time we can make this sacrifice is during the last two weeks of our tax year.

Check around town, and you will not find better prices than these. I know, because my competitors do not stock <u>half</u> my volume or selection, so they could not afford to post these discounts even at tax time.

Take a moment to examine these prices and your own business needs for the rest of the year. I will be calling you the morning of the 28th to see if we can do some last-second business at these rock bottom prices. Thank you again.

Sincerely,

John Smith

John Smith

FOLLOW-UP TO A SALES PRESENTATION

A brief, to-the-point, but friendly letter to an attendee of a sales presentation can make quite an impact. Not only does it reinforce your name and product or service in the prospect's mind, but it makes him or her feel cared for. This kind of follow-up shows professionalism and organization, and allows the prospect to relax knowing he or she has spent well-used time with a well-run company.

Tips on How to Customize Your Letter:

1. Thank the reader either at the beginning or end of the letter, or both.

2. Ask for their reaction immediately—don't dance around.

3. Restate a major selling point or two.

4. Emphasize your desire for the reader to become a satisfied customer.

5. Close with a pledge to do anything possible to satisfy the reader.

Optional Paragraphs and Phrases:

• I'm sorry I didn't get a chance to speak to you personally at the close of our meeting on _____ .

• Thank you for taking the time to listen to our presentation.

• It was a pleasure to meet with you and discuss the possibilities of a future business relationship.

• Thank you for making me feel right at home on my sales call last Wednesday. Since I'm just starting in this territory, friendly clients are always welcome.

• I'd like to reiterate some of the most important points we discussed on Wednesday.

• I want you to understand how important your patronage is to us. Please let me know if I can be of further service in any way.

• Our visit on Wednesday may not have been enough to answer all of your questions. Maybe we could meet again to finalize the arrangement.

• We appreciate the courtesy you showed in our sales visit yesterday.

• Thank you for letting me visit with you yesterday. Your friendliness and interest were appreciated.

A.B.C., Incorporated
One Main Street, U.S.A.
(555) 555-5555

Dear   :

    I really want to know what you think.

    After considering our product presentation over the last week, I am sure you have some valuable reactions.

    As I mentioned at our meeting, ABC Industries has been a leader in industrial cleaners for nearly half a century. We would like very much for you to join our ever-growing family of satisfied customers.

    Please take a few minutes to give us your opinion of our products. If for some reason our products are not what you are looking for, tell us why. We want to do whatever we can to satisfy you.

    Thank you for your cooperation.

                Sincerely,

                John Smith

Follow-up to a sales presentation

FOLLOW-UP TO A REGULAR CUSTOMER

Your best source of new business is old customers. Word-of-mouth has been proven time and time again to be the most steadfast form of advertising. Take the time to treat your regular customers with a little t.l.c. The time it takes to write a general "thank you and is there anything we can do" letter will be well worth the reputation it solidifies.

Tips on How to Customize Your Letter:

1. Set a tone of overall warmth and appreciation.

2. Thank the customer specifically for making the company what it is today.

3. Reassure the customer that he or she should feel free to contact you for any reason whatsoever.

4. Close your letter with a mention of a long and continued association.

Optional Paragraphs and Phrases:

- Thank you for being one of the cornerstones of ABC Industries.

- Without our regular customers, we would not have been able to grow and provide the increased services we do today.

- As we have told you before, we are here to serve you. Any comments, concerns, or questions you may have will be answered immediately.

- Please continue to pass along the good ideas and suggestions as you have in the past. These comments from loyal customers like you continue to improve ABC Industries.

- Again, thank you for your continued patronage. We look forward to a long and satisfying association with you.

- I drew up a list of people I could depend on, and your name was near the top.

- We want to make sure that you are satisfied.

- We want to make you more profitable.

- I was just reviewing your account, and want you to know personally how much I appreciate your business and our excellent working relationship.

A.B.C., Incorporated
One Main Street, U.S.A.
(555) 555-5555

Dear   :

     I want to let you know how much I enjoyed seeing you again
at the conference.

     It is often easy to get distracted with developing new
business or solving problem accounts. Yet I know that my
business depends on long-term, valued customers like you to
succeed.

     Your steady business, clear instructions, and excellent
payment history make my job easier and much more enjoyable.

     Rest assured that I and my staff will do everything in our
power to keep you satisfied and provide the kind of service that
will help you to maintain personal and professional success.

                              Sincerely,

                              John Smith

                              John Smith

Follow-up to a regular customer

CHAPTER

9

Building Customer Loyalty

Customers are hard to get, so do all you can to keep the ones you have. The right letter at the right time can go a long way toward keeping a customer.

The chapter on personal "goodwill" letters contains a number of customer-relations letters. Those letters, however, are not tied to specific business situations. The letters in this chapter are occasioned by particular events such as bad service, defective merchandise or receipt of an unusual order. It is difficult to draw up general rules for these letters, because they apply to special situations. Some of the letters are routine communications. Others should need to be written only on rare occasions—such as when the customer receives bad service or a defective product. These letters are *immensely important* if you want to keep the customer.

The purpose of all these letters is to keep the customer satisfied. This can be difficult if you are rejecting his request, or responding to a complaint. The best approach in such situations is to write with tact and provide as much information as you can. Let the customer know exactly how you reached the decision, so he can either understand the problem from your perspective or provide additional information. Always state that you are ready to change the decision if convincing information or reasons are provided.

Customer-relations letters should carry an air of friendship and cooperation. The customer should feel that he is valuable enough to you that you will do whatever is reasonable to continue the business relationship.

ACKNOWLEDGING RECEIPT OF A COMPLAINT

None of us likes to make a mistake, but none of us goes through life error-free. It's very important to good customer relations to acknowledge errors made by your company. Ignoring, denying, or covering up an obvious error can severely damage your reputation. The customer will most appreciate an admission and a proposed solution. His or her faith in your company will then go unshaken.

Tips on How to Customize Your Letter:

1. Acknowledge first the receipt of the customer's complaint. He or she will feel "heard."

2. Make it very clear that you are doing your best to remedy the situation.

3. Tell the reader to rest easy; the matter is in your hands and is being taken care of.

4. End the letter with an apology and an indication of future follow-up.

Optional Paragraphs and Phrases:

• Please accept our apologies for the serious error described in your letter of _____ .

• The error should, of course, never have occurred to begin with. However, since it exists we will do everything in our power to remedy it as quickly as possible.

• We have received your letter of _____ . Your customer service representative, Jane Brown, is on vacation. I have started the procedure to correct the situation in her absence. Jane will be in contact with you when she returns on _____ .

• Again, we are so sorry for any inconvenience. Please let us know if there is anything else we can do to ease the situation.

• We can understand why you are upset about being without a _____ for several weeks.

• I always regret those occasions when a customer says he is not entirely satisfied with our service.

• The manufacturer already has started work on your replacement parts. The plant was closed for a few weeks, but your parts are among the first ones being completed. You should have them within a month.

• I know how frustrating it is when a major purchase doesn't live up to your expectations.

• We take many precautions to see that mistakes such as this do not happen. As long as human beings are involved, however, there will be a small number of errors. I assure you that these errors are very rare and hope you will accept our apology.

• We have received your letter of _____ and are presently looking into the situation.

• Thank you for bringing your problem to our attention.

A.B.C., Incorporated
One Main Street, U.S.A.
(555) 555-5555

Dear   :

    I have received your letter dated September 17.

    Since the letter describes a serious error which you no doubt would expect to have been resolved by now, I am personally investigating the situation to determine what happened.

    You can rest assured that I will do my best to resolve this situation to our mutual satisfaction and ensure that it does not happen again.

    I am sorry for any inconvenience this may have caused you. We will contact you as soon as the matter has been resolved.

                 Sincerely,

                 John Smith
                 John Smith

Acknowledging receipt of a complaint

LETTERS AGREEING WITH A CUSTOMER'S COMPLAINT

When a customer is right, a customer is right! And when a customer is right, the best thing for the business at fault to do is to admit to its error and try to redeem itself. A simple, straightforward apology with a plan of how amends are to be made usually does the trick.

Tips on How to Customize Your Letter:

1. Say right away what the error was and how it will be remedied.

2. Apologize for the error and explain your understanding of it.

3. State a positive fact about the situation—like, the shipment is on its way.

4. Offer some kind of repayment to the customer for their trouble (discount, gratis product, dinner, free sample).

5. End the letter on an apologetic, but positive note.

Optional Paragraphs and Phrases:

• I have looked into the situation described in your letter of _____ .

• The problem, from my understanding, stems from our shipping department.

• We are so sorry you had to experience any inconvenience connected with our product.

• We have begun to establish some organizational changes to make positively certain this type of mistake will not happen again.

• I have personally witnessed the shipment of your order.

• There will be no charge to you for your order, of course.

• Thank you for bringing the situation to my attention and for being so patient.

• Letters such as yours of _____ , are one of the ways we can work to perfect our operation. Thank you.

• I am sorry you felt it necessary to go to another vendor.

• Let me assure you that the same error will not happen again.

• Allow us to redeem ourselves by replacing the damaged product free of charge and paying for any repairs. Send us all your bills and invoices related to the incident.

• Again, accept my apologies on behalf of ABC, Inc., and please give our product a second chance in the future.

A.B.C., Incorporated
One Main Street, U.S.A.
(555) 555-5555

Dear   :

    I have carefully reviewed your letter of September 17 and collected enough information to reach a conclusion.

    It is obvious that you were billed for goods we did not ship. I have had our accountant review our flow of paperwork, and already we have instituted several changes that should ensure such a mistake does not happen again.

    The goods you ordered are finally on their way. We have enclosed an extra case of supplies with my compliments and apology. Thank you for bringing this problem to our attention.

                Sincerely,

                John Smith

                John Smith

Agreeing with a customer's
complaint — correcting error

A.B.C., Incorporated
One Main Street, U.S.A.
(555) 555-5555

Dear   :

    Thank you for bringing your auto service problem to my attention. The best way we can avoid future problems is by getting this type of feedback if a situation occurs.

    As I understand matters, you engaged another firm to handle the original repair that was unresolved after we worked on it.

    Considering the circumstances, I would like to regain your confidence by crediting your account with us in the amount of our original invoice of $, or if you prefer, issue you a refund.

    We do excellent work as a rule and have the best reputation on the east coast.

    My apologies for the inconvenience this particular situation caused you.

               Sincerely,

               John Smith

               John Smith

LETTERS DISAGREEING WITH A CUSTOMER'S COMPLAINTS

Diplomacy and tact are your best resources in handling an irate customer's complaint. When the problem lies outside your company's responsibility, it can require even more careful correspondence than usual. Above all, you want to avoid defensiveness and present a response that helps customers feel you care and are assisting with the problem. Preserve the buyer/seller association by applying the tips below.

Tips on How to Customize Your Letter:

1. Be straightforward, but as diplomatic and polite as possible.

2. Express concern over the damage or complaint situation.

3. Clearly explain how the situation has been researched and your understanding of it.

4. Explain your position firmly and stick by it.

5. End the letter on a positive, helpful note.

Optional Paragraphs and Phrases:

• Please accept our apologies for the damaged shipment you received on _____ .

• Thank you for bringing your problem to our attention.

• We have completed a thorough investigation of the situation and have found the error not to be with our organization. Let me explain...

• Please let me know if I can be of any assistance in finding the cause of the error.

• In your owner's manual on page four there is a warning not to use leaded gasoline in this machine. Occasionally a customer misses this warning, so we have tried emphasizing it in the manual.

• Our laboratory analysis and that of an outside expert indicated that this damage was caused by the machine's being dropped. Such damage is not ordinary wear and tear, and therefore is not covered under the warranty.

- The information you submitted indicates that you initially took the product to an unauthorized dealer for repairs. Our products have several unique features, and special training is required to repair them properly. That is why we guarantee only machines repaired by authorized dealers and cannot warranty damage that occurs after work is done by an unauthorized dealer.

- We will be happy to repair the damage, but we would have to bill you for such repairs. We estimate that the repairs will cost around $75. Please let us know if you want us to make the repairs or ship the product to you as it is.

- No doubt this result is not all you would like it to be, but we hope you can understand why no other result is possible.

- If we have overlooked or misunderstood something, do not hesitate to let me know.

- We do everything possible to keep a customer satisfied. But in this instance, we've gone as far as we can go on the customer's behalf.

A.B.C., Incorporated
One Main Street, U.S.A.
(555) 555-5555

Dear   :

    We were sorry to hear that the glassware we shipped to you
was damaged by the time it reached you.

    A check of our records reveals that the shipper acknowledged
receiving the glassware intact and signed a receipt to that
effect. The terms of our sales are "FOB shipper." Therefore,
you will need to take your complaint directly to the shipper.

    If you have any trouble reaching a satisfactory agreement
with the shipper, please let us know. We send a fairly large
amount of orders through this shipper and probably can exert some
leverage on your behalf.

    Please tell us if there is anything else we can do.

                    Sincerely,

                    John Smith

                    John Smith

Disagreeing with a customer's complaint —
problem outside your responsibility

A.B.C., Incorporated
One Main Street, U.S.A.
(555) 555-5555

Dear   :

   We have received your letter of October 17 and regret hearing that your transmission failed during a recent business trip only six months after we replaced it.

   We are fully prepared to stand behind our guarantee and reimburse anyone who incurs additional expenses after we worked on their car. In reviewing the invoices you submitted to us, however, we noticed that your car has been driven over 15,000 miles in the 6 months since we repaired it. Our guarantee lasts for one year or 10,000 miles, whichever comes first.

   Therefore we cannot reimburse you for the transmission repair. We offer the longest repair guarantee in this area and give our customers the benefit of the doubt whenever possible. But in this case we are clearly not liable for the additional expenses.

   Considering the number of miles you drive each year, we suggest you have your car thoroughly checked out at least three times a year and particularly before long trips. We hope you will consider us the next time your car needs work done.

                              Sincerely,

                              John Smith

                              John Smith

LETTER APOLOGIZING FOR AN EMPLOYEE'S ACTION

Business owners would all like to have perfect employees. Unfortunately, no matter how careful you are in your hiring policies, you still cannot do away with human error or the few bad apples that turn up in any organization. This letter, written well, can make the difference between a soothed customer and a seething ex-customer.

Tips on How to Customize Your Letter:

1. Thank the customer immediately for bringing the matter to your attention.

2. Restate the specific circumstance for which you are apologizing (no use signing a blank apology).

3. Clearly explain the actions to be taken to try to remedy the situation.

4. Try not to blame or speak harshly of the individual employee. This shows strife within your organization, which can be disconcerting to the customer.

5. Always close a letter of this nature with a wish for their continued patronage and forgiveness.

Optional Paragraphs and Phrases:

• Thank you for your letter of _____ explaining the incident you experienced in our downtown store on _____ .

• Please accept my personal apologies and those of the entire company for the sloppy work of our technician.

• I hope that you suffered no irreparable damage or embarrassment as a result.

• I have looked into the matter myself and have called upon the services of our National Customer Service Manager _____ , to thoroughly investigate the situation and take the appropriate corrective action.

• The employee you encountered has been severely reprimanded, and now understands that conduct of this type cannot and will not be tolerated.

• Again, please accept our apologies and assurance that such an incident will never happen again.

• Please remember that your patronage is invaluable to us.

• We always appreciate hearing about such incidents so that we can investigate them and take all appropriate actions.

• Your letter is in the hands of our personnel department which will certainly take appropriate action. In the meantime, please accept my personal apology for any unpleasantness you experienced as a result of the incident.

• A firm with a large amount of transactions inevitably will make some mistakes. But there is no reason for the employees of any size firm to be rude or abusive to customers.

• We value your patronage and hope you will realize that this is an isolated incident that will not occur again in this firm.

A.B.C., Incorporated
One Main Street, U.S.A.
(555) 555-5555

Dear   :

    Thank you for telling me about the unpleasant incident you were subjected to while I was on vacation last week. Please accept my apologies for my assistant manager's behavior.

    I have thoroughly discussed the incident with the assistant manager and am sure that it will not happen again. During my vacation things got unusually hectic here, and you happened to be in the wrong place at the wrong time.

    This is no excuse for what happened, of course. But I thought you should know that my assistant does not usually behave that way and was under a great deal of pressure at the time.

    I am grateful for your patronage and hope you will accept my apology for this incident.

                Sincerely,

                John Smith

                John Smith

Letter apologizing for
an employee's action

GENERAL LETTER OF APOLOGY

While every business receives complaints from customers, some are valid and some are not. Whether the customer is right or wrong, they are unhappy when they complain, and need to hear from you to be made happy again. Hence, there is the general letter of apology to soothe the malcontented client in non-specific terms to either prevent self-indictment on your part or to give you time to look more thoroughly into the situation.

Tips on How to Customize Your Letter:

1. Express your thanks to the reader for taking the time to write and notify you of his or her complaint.

2. Explain what you see of the situation.

3. If the customer has a valid point, apologize and reassure him or her that measures are being taken to correct the situation.

4. If the customer does not have a valid point, apologize for their discomfort and dissatisfaction. Then explain gently how you cannot be responsible for the situation.

5. Whether the reader is right or wrong, offer some small token to ease their inconvenience, if at all possible.

Optional Paragraphs and Phrases:

• I sincerely regret the condition you received your package in, and hope the replacement we are sending will be satisfactory.

• Thank you for taking your valuable time to let me know about the problem with your equipment.

• We always appreciate hearing from our customers. We do, however, wish that you had been completely satisfied with your order.

• Please accept our apologies for any inconvenience you have experienced.

• We are so sorry to have you, one of our most valued customers, dissatisfied in any way.

• We are very sorry for the delay in receipt of your package. Our records do show that it was shipped in a timely manner, and the courier service was negligent in its duties. We have changed couriers to avoid this type of situation in the future. Please accept the enclosed discount coupon as our gift for your inconvenience.

- I am sorry that you have suffered any inconvenience at all. Unfortunately, the company that installs your equipment works completely independently from our company. We have, however, passed along a copy of your letter to the installation company in order for them to remedy the situation as soon as possible. The person you may want to talk to at that company is _____ . Please let us know if something is not done right away to correct the installation.

- Please be sure to think of us when you next need industrial cleansers or equipment. We will do everything in our power to make your next experience with us a perfect one.

- Again, thank you for writing, and let us know if we can be of service in any other way.

A.B.C., Incorporated
One Main Street, U.S.A.
(555) 555-5555

Dear   :

    Thank you for your recent letter, in which you point out that it takes about four weeks for a product to reach a customer after it has been ordered. We can grow and prosper only by responding to useful criticisms such as yours.

    We are sorry if the shipping time caused you problems. In the meantime we are exploring alternatives that will allow us to fulfill orders faster without increasing costs appreciably.

        Sincerely,

        John Smith

        John Smith

General letter of apology

ACKNOWLEDGEMENT OF AN ORDER

Very important to good customer service and relations is a polite acknowledgement of an order. Once a customer places an order, he or she would like to know if it has been received before actually receiving the merchandise. These acknowledgement letters are also a good way to ensure proper communication between your company and its customers. These letters are good vehicles for pertinent information, such as an unavoidable shipment delay, or a quick sales pitch for an upcoming sale or new product.

Tips on How to Customize Your Letters:

1. Be polite and businesslike.

2. Document all necessary facts and/or instructions clearly in the letter. This will cut down on unnecessary calls from the customers.

3. Acknowledge the exact order and the method of payment.

4. Support the customer's decision at the close of the letter. Let him or her know you feel they've made a good decision.

Optional Paragraphs and Phrases:

• Thank you for your order for six _____ paid through your MasterCard account # _____ . We welcome you as a new ABC, Inc. client.

• Thank you for your large order of industrial cleansers and the check you enclosed with it.

• We want to let you know that we have a 20% discount in effect on the items you ordered. We will, of course, process your order with the discount and mail you a refund check for the difference right away.

• Just to keep you up-to-date on what's happening at ABC, Inc., we want to notify you of our new line of high efficiency cleaning equipment coming out this fall.

- Remember, for your spring shopping, we will be having our annual clearance sales starting in February and running through May.

- Thank you for your order! We are sending out all items except the Model 413 which is on back order. We apologize for the delay and any inconvenience it may cause you. Please rest assured that we will send you our Model 413 by special courier as soon as it arrives in our warehouse, which should be within the next week.

- Just to let you know that your decision to purchase the Model 212 was a good one, we have been receiving letters by the hundreds from satisfied customers who have been using the same model for the past few months.

- Again, welcome to our family of satisfied customers. We are confident that you will be extremely pleased with your new equipment. Let us know how we can help you in the future.

Optional Paragraphs and Phrases:

- Your order is currently being processed and should be delivered within 10 days.

- Response to our recent offer far exceeded our expectations. While this is gratifying, it will result in delays in fulfilling your order.

- To compensate you for the delay, we are including a special bonus with your order.

- We have received your order and set aside the goods you requested. Unfortunately, we cannot ship goods without a 50% deposit on the purchase price.

- While looking over your recent order, it occurred to me that you might be interested in another of our products.

A.B.C., Incorporated
One Main Street, U.S.A.
(555) 555-5555

Dear   :

    Thank you very much for your order dated June 22. I really enjoy getting new business from you after such a long interval.

    To confirm, you ordered   number of   and have charged your   account for the full amount of $.

    Most of your order is on hand and has been fulfilled already. You should receive the shipment within ten days from today.

    The computer diskettes, however, must be ordered from the manufacturer and will take another week or so. We are sorry for the delay, but the sale we ran on this item generated far more orders than we dared hope for. I think you will agree that the savings is well worth the wait.

    We appreciate your order and hope to receive more in the future.

            Sincerely,

            John Smith

Acknowledging an order — back order

A.B.C., Incorporated
One Main Street, U.S.A.
(555) 555-5555

Dear   :

    We were glad to receive your order dated August 21
for   number of   .

    Unfortunately, we cannot ship orders to a post office box.
To better track delivery, we ship all orders via United Parcel
Service and therefore need a street address.

    Your order is processed and ready for a new address to be
put on the label. You should receive the package shortly after
we receive your street address.

    Thank you again for your order. We are confident that you
will be more than satisfied with your decision.

                Sincerely,

                John Smith

                John Smith

Acknowledging an order —
explaining shipment procedures

LETTER ANNOUNCING A PRICE INCREASE

A price increase is never good news to the ears of customers, but it is a necessity to business. The way you break the news to your customers is crucial to whether they loyally stick by you or whether they start comparison shopping among your competitors.

Tips on How to Customize Your Letter:

1. Express the price increase as a necessary evil; something you were trying to avoid for your customers' sakes, but just couldn't any longer.

2. Give some specific reasons for the increase, but don't go into the company's entire financial history.

3. Sympathize with the customer by expressing the fact that you are in the same boat with your suppliers, which is one of the reasons for the increase.

4. Close with an expression of the value this customer has to your company and a vow to keep prices as low as possible in the future.

Optional Paragraphs and Phrases:

• It's always difficult to announce a price increase, but I'm afraid the time has come when ABC Industries must do so.

• Not all of our products have gone up in price. Please note the new price list enclosed for the specific adjustments.

• I hope you can understand that while we try our hardest to keep a good long distance between increases, the cost of goods just catches up with us from time to time.

• We at ABC Industries can sympathize with how you feel about the rising costs these days. In fact the increases our suppliers have been incorporating into their bills is one of the reasons we were forced to increase our prices.

• I'm sure you know by now how much we value your patronage. Please believe us when we say that one of our ongoing goals is to provide the best products and service at the lowest prices for our clients. This recent increase does not in any way mean that we are deserting that goal. In fact, we hope not to have to write a letter of this type for many years to come.

A.B.C., Incorporated
One Main Street, U.S.A.
(555) 555-5555

Dear   :

     We held off as long as we could. We just can't wait
any longer. It's hard for me to announce this, but we must
raise our prices starting one month from today. The specific
increases are stated on the enclosed price list.

     I know many people don't understand how we can raise
prices when the government says inflation is down. But you
probably know as well as I do that while prices on consumer
goods such as food and fuel are declining, the prices of
business supplies and services are steadily rising.

     In the last few months, I've received several announce-
ments just like this one. We want to stay competitive and
keep all our customers, so we absorbed these price increases
whenever we could. Regrettably, we now must pass these costs
on to you.

     I'm sure you know how much we value you as a customer
and that this action is a last resort. We have done and
will do everything we can to keep our prices as competitive
as possible.

                              Sincerely,

                              John Smith
                              John Smith

*Letter announcing a
price increase*

NOTIFYING CUSTOMERS OF A MOVE

Notifying a customer of a move is a crucial piece of correspondence. This letter must be sent out with plenty of lead time so the customers can prepare for your move. People get easily accustomed to locations and routines. Give your customers time to get used to the idea of your business move. You may also consider writing two letters about one month apart; the first on your current stationery, the second on stationery with your new address.

Tips on How to Customize Your Letter:

1. Open the letter with a positive reason for the move.

2. Explain how the move will benefit the customer as well as the business.

3. End the letter on a friendly, personal note.

4. Close with thanks for the customer's loyalty and patience during the move.

Optional Paragraphs and Phrases:

• We are taking advantage of the glorious new industrial park on the outskirts of town and moving our business!

• We're bursting at the seams! So, we've decided to have new offices built. The new location will be: _____ .

• Our new site will provide more room for demonstrating products, more efficient shipping facilities, and more parking for you!

• We expect far fewer letters commenting on the limited parking!

• I want to thank you for your patronage over the years, which has played a big part in allowing us to expand.

• Please be patient with us for the month it will take us to settle into the new location. After that you will be amazed at the increased efficiency and streamlined organization, we promise!

A.B.C., Incorporated
One Main Street, U.S.A.
(555) 555-5555

Dear   :

It finally happened! Thanks to good customers such as you, we finally outgrew our old quarters. We will be moving effective October 1.

The new offices will give us more room and allow us to be organized more efficiently. We believe this will show up in better service to you.

We look forward to serving you from our new "home" very shortly.

Sincerely,

John Smith

John Smith

*Notifying customers of
a move*

ANNOUNCING NEW PRODUCTS TO VALUED CUSTOMERS

This letter could just as well have been filed in the Sales Letter Section of this book. The proper, and timely announcement of a new product and/or service can be a most valuable sales tool. In fact, it can trigger an avalanche of word-of-mouth sales. Be sure to announce all new products and/or services, in the format of a letter, formal announcement card, or press release, approximately 2 months prior to their release on the market. You may consider follow-up letters after the original announcement, and even hold special sales or public relations functions to christen the new addition.

Tips on How to Customize Your Letter:

1. Make your customer feel honored to be receiving the announcement.

2. Express the announcement as a service to the customer.

3. Let the reader know that you are making the announcement to him or her significantly ahead of the general public announcement.

4. Explain the benefits of the new product or service briefly.

5. Close the letter with a special offer or discount for the customer and thanks for their continued patronage.

Optional Paragraphs and Phrases:

• We wanted you, one of our favorite customers, to be among the first to know of our latest Model 513.

• You are hearing about this innovation a full month before the general public, which is a full two months before it is on the marketplace.

• Since you already use the 413, you can see from the enclosed brochure how the 513 can better and more quickly fill your needs.

• We are offering a special, trade-in discount for present owners of the 413.

• Again, thank you for your loyal patronage which allows us to continue bringing forth the most current equipment available.

• As a regular customer of our line of 14-karat jewelry, you'd be interested to know that we can now pass on a most unusual savings to you. With gold now trading at only $320 per ounce, that means we can deliver finished fashion jewelry to you at only 15% above spot gold prices, or only about $12 per gram of gold. This far below our retail price...

• It's that time of year again: time for personalized business calendars for 1989, with your firm's name embossed on each page—gently reminding your customers where to do business each month. Order 100 copies now, and they're available for as little as $5.50 each.

A.B.C., Incorporated
One Main Street, U.S.A.
(555) 555-5555

Dear   :

    We believe in treating our most valued <u>old</u> customers as if
they were our most sought-after <u>new</u> customers. Therefore, we
make it a policy to give you advance notice of our best new
products, new services, and our lowest bargain prices.

    Because of our concern for putting your needs first, I am
writing you this letter a full month before we announce a phe-
nomenal new product to the marketplace: the gravity-induction
silver reclamation filter. As a long-time user of our previous
models, you can see the immediate benefits of this new product
over the old methods of reclaiming silver from your high-volume
photographic processing.

    Before we announce this product to the marketplace, we are
offering it to our very best customers, like you, for an unprece-
dented 15 percent off the retail price. Consult the enclosed
brochure for more details. I will be calling on you soon to see
if this is the right product for you. Production is just beginning, and we can reserve one of the very first copies for you.

            Sincerely,

            John Smith

            John Smith

*Announcing new products to
valued customers*

CHAPTER 10

Making the Most of the Media

Letters to the media generally serve the purpose of generating free publicity for the writer and his business.

The media is an untapped source of free advertising for many businesses. Journalists like nothing better than having a story presented to them instead of their having to go out and find the stories. Properly produced letters and press releases can generate a lot of favorable attention for every business. And, if a story is published, the effect on sales can be incredible!

To exploit the media for your business, you must first stage a media event. Such events include opening or moving a business, celebrating an anniversary, and receiving or giving an award or commendation. Virtually anything you do outside of normal day-to-day business activities is a potential media event.

Letters and releases to the media should be concise, fact-filled, authoritative, complete, and objective. Any letter or release sent to the media will be heavily edited before it is used, but the chances of getting free media exposure are directly related to the extent to which the original document resembles an actual news or feature article. Perhaps the most important part of the media event letter is the follow-up. Once you've made the commitment to stir up the media, follow through and make sure your story is told!

Correcting stories about your business or industry can be essential to your success. Many businesses have been made or broken by media exposure. While the odds are low that a particular business will have to oppose a media campaign against it, most businesses will face situations where incorrect information is printed about their firms or industries. In either case, letters to the media are necessary and must be carefully written.

RESPONSES TO EDITORIALS—POSITIVE AND NEGATIVE

As often as business owners want to be in the media for publicity and subsequent sales, the media can be detrimental if something or someone is misrepresented.

Tips on How to Customize Your Letters:

1. Start off immediately with the fact that there was an error.

2. Enumerate the mistakes if more than one. If you are concerned about only one error, explain in detail what the mistake was.

3. State clearly what you feel the ramifications of such an error will be.

4. Demand a retraction or an apology or both if it is appropriate.

More Useful Paragraphs:

• Although I appreciate the article about my company, ABC Inc., you wrongly misquoted me in paragraph 3.

• I have found more than several errors in your article on nuclear waste. They are as follows:

• The extent of the errors and the vast quantity of them in one article drastically reduces my trust in you as a reporter and in your newspaper as a vehicle of communication of facts.

• The quote you used could feasibly destroy my reputation as an industrial supplier.

• I hope to read an extensive correction of the article in tomorrow's paper.

• I feel it is my right to demand a retraction of this misquote, and I so do.

A.B.C., Incorporated
One Main Street, U.S.A.
(555) 555-5555

Dear   :

    We are very pleased with your report on last night's news-cast about Clarence Thompson, who was just elected CEO of ABC, Inc. Your report was accurate and comprehensive.

    Mr. Thompson has been associated with ABC, Inc., since its beginning. He has continuously aided in the growth and improvement of not only our company but the community as well. We are happy you chose to publicize this noted citizen.

    Your report is potentially helpful to our business--we have had several calls about it already. We are looking forward to assisting you in future newscasts. Thank you again.

                                Sincerely,

                                John Smith

                                John Smith

Response to editorial — positive

A.B.C., Incorporated
One Main Street, U.S.A.
(555) 555-5555

Dear   :

We discovered several errors and misleading statements in your January 15 editorial entitled "Cleaning Up Day Care." These statements misinform the public and lead to poor public policy decisions.

Only a small percentage of day-care facilities have the problems mentioned in your article. These problem facilities must be improved or closed down but not by imposing heavy burdens on well-run facilities and their clients.

Strong regulations would not solve the problems you mention. Instead, regulations would drive up the cost of day-care services, drive many small centers out of business, and reduce the number of options available to parents. Regulations would deprive many parents of affordable day-care services, not ensure everyone of quality, low-cost services.

The problems encountered at some day-care centers are not the result of too little government involvement. Rather they are the result of too little parental involvement. Our center, for instance, belongs to a regional council of day-care facilities. We subscribe to a code of ethics that is distributed to each child's parent and must meet a number of minimum operating standards before joining the council. In addition, the council handles all complaints about members and keeps a file of all complaints that is available to inquiring parents.

Sincerely,

John Smith

John Smith

Response to editorial — negative

LETTERS AND PRESS RELEASES SUGGESTING MEDIA EVENTS

The media is always hungry for news, so why not give it to them and get some free publicity at the same time? Be sure to announce, either in letter or press release form any event in your company that you feel is newsworthy. Consider: moves of the business, new products, guest speakers, new employees, promoted employees, anniversaries of your business's founding, or acquisitions. A letter is the more appropriate format when either you know the reader personally, or your news item is of specific interest to a particular person or group and not to general readership. On the other hand, a press release is better used when contacting a publication or other media in which you may know a "name" but not a "person" personally. Releases also announce events of interest to larger groups and markets.

How to Customize Your Letter or Press Release:

1. Keep in mind that you are trying to generate sales through this publicity. Approach media that will be interested in your event, but also those that reach the largest portions of your market.

2. Choose your format based on the recipient. If you have a specific person you wish to contact, use the personal letter approach. If on the other hand you want your idea to go to the city desk, or you're not sure who it should go to, use a press release.

3. State your news item upfront, because very often media people don't read past the middle of the page.

4. Show enthusiasm and make it clear, either in fact or embellishment, why the media should include the item in their show or paper.

5. Press releases should look different than letters. Type them on your letterhead, but make sure they are double-spaced.

Optional Paragraphs and Phrases:

The subject of these types of letters is usually too specialized to offer much help in additional paragraphs. Instead, we have provided you with seven examples to use as idea stimulators. Take your own topic, follow the tips listed above, and use these examples as models. Then do your own thing and watch the publicity roll in!

A.B.C., Incorporated
One Main Street, U.S.A.
(555) 555-5555

Dear Editor:

    The president has established Wednesday, November 17, as American Enterprise Day. The president's action is designed to remind Americans of the vital, positive role American enterprise, particularly small business enterprise, has played in the development of this country.

    I am writing to suggest that you do a feature story on American Enterprise Day by featuring local businesses that represent exactly what the president had in mind when he proclaimed American Enterprise Day.

    As owner of a local small business, I can recommend several businesses for you to profile. Of course, I believe my own firm would be ideal for inclusion in the article. Information on my firm is enclosed.

    I am prepared to assist you in the preparation of this article in any way I can. I will follow up this letter by telephoning you in about ten days and asking for your reactions to this idea.

    I look forward to speaking with you.

Sincerely,

John Smith

John Smith

Media event letter —
business—related holiday

A.B.C., Incorporated
One Main Street, U.S.A.
(555) 555-5555

Dear   :

Enclosed is a review copy of my recently published book, <u>How To Buy a Business</u>. I have been a small business consultant in this area for six years and have helped numerous local entrepreneurs buy their own businesses.

I think this would be a good topic for the "People Are Talking" show. My experience in this city convinces me that a number of people are interested in buying a business. The statistics I cite in Chapter 1 of my book support this. I think the viewer call-in part of the show would be particularly lively.

As you can tell from the Table of Contents of the book, I cover every aspect of buying a business. Based on the demographics of your audience, I believe the topics in the first three chapters would be ideal for the interview session: Why to buy a business, where to find a business for sale, and how to finance a business purchase.

To aid you in your decision, I am enclosing:

*biographical information

*a description of my business

*a press release from my publisher

Since I am based in this area, I can appear almost any time.

I will be calling you in about ten days to further discuss this idea with you.

Sincerely,

John Smith

John Smith

Media event letter —
recently published book

A.B.C., Incorporated
One Main Street, U.S.A.
(555) 555-5555

Dear   :

ABC, Inc., a fast-growing Des Moines publisher, is celebrating its third anniversary by moving into spacious offices in the new downtown office mall.

ABC started operations three years ago at its present headquarters in East Des Moines. In the last three years the firm has successfully published five books and three periodicals.

The firm's most successful product has been its second book, Save a Fortune, written by publisher Donald Lant. The book, now in its fourth printing, sold over 20,000 copies in the two years since it was first published and received favorable reviews in a number of leading consumer and business publications.

The Mutual Fund Guide is the firm's most successful periodical. This comprehensive, monthly review of mutual funds worldwide publishes the performance of over 1,500 mutual funds and provides a detailed review of two funds per issue. A number of professional investors and financial counselors subscribe to the publication and regularly use it to make investment decisions.

ABC is moving into the new quarters because its present offices cannot comfortably house its 45 employees. Lant believes the firm's publications will be improved by the new location in the heart of the downtown business community.

Sincerely,

John Smith

John Smith

Media event letter — anniversary

A.B.C., Incorporated
One Main Street, U.S.A.
(555) 555-5555

Date:
FOR IMMEDIATE RELEASE

DES MOINES, IOWA -- A fast growing Des Moines publisher is celebrating its third anniversary by moving into spacious offices in the new downtown office mall.

ABC, Inc. started operations three years ago, and has since successfully published five books and three periodicals.

Save a Fortune by Donald Lant, the firm's second book, has been its most successful to date. Now in its fourth printing, the book has sold over 20,000 copies in the last two years.

ABC's most successful periodical is the Mutual Fund Guide, a comprehensive, monthly review of mutual funds worldwide. It publishes the performances of over 1,500 mutual funds and provides a detailed review of two funds per issue.

A number of professional investors and financial counselors subscribe to the Mutual Fund Guide and use it regularly to make investment decisions.

ABC is moving into its new quarters because the present ABC offices cannot comfortably house the 45 employees of the company. Lant, author of Save a Fortune and owner of ABC, Inc., believes the firm's publications will be improved by the new location in the heart of the downtown business community.

FOR MORE INFORMATION, CONTACT:

Press release — anniversary

Note: This release covers the same topic as the letter on page 197. There are certain situations where both formats need to be used.

A.B.C., Incorporated
One Main Street, U.S.A.
(555) 555-5555

Date:
FOR IMMEDIATE RELEASE

Frank Atkinson, president of Richmond-based Cavalier Associates, Inc., will address the annual Virginia Entrepreneurs
Association Convention this Saturday at 8 p.m. at the Hyatt
Regency. Mr. Atkinson will speak on how to find and develop an
effective small business idea.

In an interview with...[name of newspaper], Atkinson said
that the entrepreneur is the backbone of the American economy.
"Government statistics show that most new jobs are created by
small businesses that are less than five years old," Atkinson
added.

Interest in starting and operating a small business has
increased dramatically in the last few years. Atkinson believes
many people are turning to entrepreneurship because small business ownership is the best way to achieve financial independence
and substantial wealth.

"Periodically Americans blame business as some sort of evil
force," said Atkinson, "but after a few years people realize that
both personal and national fortunes depend on business." In the
last few years Americans have moved rapidly from an anti-business
stance to a pro-enterprise position, according to Atkinson.

In his speech to the VEA, Atkinson will list the 18 best
sources for new business ideas, tell how to determine if a
particular idea is right for you and explain how an idea can be
turned into an operating business.

--More--

Press release — speaking engagement

A.B.C., Incorporated
One Main Street, U.S.A.
(555) 555-5555

Atkinson says his speech is based largely on personal experience. The 45-year-old entrepreneur has founded or co-founded 11 small businesses and counseled others in establishing numerous others. Atkinson says not all of his businesses were successful, and his speaking and counseling are designed to keep others from making the same mistakes he did.

FOR MORE INFORMATION, CONTACT:

A.B.C., Incorporated
One Main Street, U.S.A.
(555) 555-5555

Date:
FOR IMMEDIATE RELEASE

ABC, Inc., Breaks Ground on New Office Complex

Anytown, USA--R. Donald Harris, Chairman of the Board of ABC, Inc., a leading engineering firm in the area, beamed broadly as he broke ground on his company's new office complex on East Third Street. As photographers captured the event, over 150 visiting business people and civic leaders applauded the first shovelful of dirt lifted from the five-acre site just off the Main Street business complex.

The new ABC headquarters is the largest new building contract awarded in the Anytown area since 1981. With over 120,000 square feet, it will house 450 full-time employees, a large computer complex, and a projected 100 new job openings in the next 18 months, Chairman Harris said. Plans for an administration annex are already on the drawing boards if these growth figures are exceeded.

ABC, Inc., specializes in industrial equipment and supplies. The building contract was awarded to Harlan Sanders & Sons, a local construction firm with numerous local business buildings to their credit.

FOR MORE INFORMATION, CONTACT:

Press release — new office complex

A.B.C., Incorporated
One Main Street, U.S.A.
(555) 555-5555

Date:
FOR IMMEDIATE RELEASE

Mutual Fund Manager Scores Five-Year 150 Percent Track Record

Anytown, USA--R. Donald Samples, director of ABC, Inc., Anytown, has established an enviable five-year track record of more than 150 percent growth in a market which has "only" grown 38 percent in the same five years.

"Our strategy is conservative growth with income, making this 150 percent figure all the more amazing," said Samples. "Normally, a speculative fund, or gold fund, can generate such results in a bull market, but seldom do you find a conservative growth fund achieving such a top track record."

When asked for his secret, Samples says, "No secret. I just read and apply the classic security analysis theories of Benjamin Graham. It's as 'easy' as plugging in his old formulas to the new market." Of course, it's "Not really that easy," he grins, "or everybody would be doing it."

ABC, Inc., has over $200 million in capitalization with over 15,000 investors worldwide. The recent success has brought Samples more business than he can handle. "We're staffing up to meet demand, but right now we have more phone messages than employees to handle them. By this time next month, however, we will have the staff to handle demand." Most businessmen would welcome such "problems."

--More--

Press release — growth achievement

A.B.C., Incorporated
One Main Street, U.S.A.
(555) 555-5555

Originally working out of his home on evenings and weekends, while working days for a major brokerage firm, Samples now employs five full-time research assistants. He hopes to double his staff in six months and align his funds with one of the "majors" on the East Coast. For now, he won't reveal which major brokerage firm is courting him, but he says, "expect an announcement within 60 days."

FOR MORE INFORMATION, CONTACT:

A.B.C., Incorporated
One Main Street, U.S.A.
(555) 555-5555

Date:
FOR IMMEDIATE RELEASE

ABC, Inc., Hires New Director

Anytown, USA--ABC, Inc., has announced the hiring of
J. Michael Simpson, former insurance commissioner, as director of
their small but growing firm.

Simpson, 53, grew through the ranks of life insurance for 20
years, up to the senior vice president level, before accepting
the political appointment in neighboring Louisiana. After
resigning at the end of Governor David Treen's term (1980-84),
Simpson considered offers from many major insurance firms before
accepting the top post at the local independent.

"I prefer to be captain of a small, growing company than
first mate on a big ship with a clearly charted path," Simpson
said, a champion yachtsman, obviously showing his love of
sailing. "We have the opportunity to build ABC into one of this
state's premier independent firms. The management team has
already met with me and drafted a five-year growth plan toward
that end. I'm excited with the team that built ABC up to this
point, and I'm sure we can work together toward greater growth in
the future."

ABC, Inc., located at One Main Street, has over 100 agents
and 200 total employees in the Anytown area, with independent
agents representing them throughout the five-state Gulf region.

FOR MORE INFORMATION, CONTACT:

FOLLOW-UP LETTER TO A JOURNALIST

Nothing is so frustrating as suggesting an interview for an article or radio or TV show and then hearing nothing. A quick follow-up letter to the person writing the article or the producer of the show can never hurt, and will probably get things moving.

Tips on How to Customize Your Letter:

1. Remind the journalist of your idea and the specifics of what it was about.

2. Tell him that you have attempted to contact him, but with no luck.

3. Emphasize the timeliness of the subject, and tell him that you'll be back!

More Useful Paragraphs:

• I really enjoyed talking to you last month about a suggested show on how a basement business grew to the size of an industrial park.

• I was looking forward to reading the article long before this. What happened?

• Please let me know the status of the project I suggested, as we have had some drastic changes here which I think might make an interesting addition if the article is still alive.

• I look forward to hearing from you soon. If I don't, I will be calling, because I am anxious to hear what has happened.

A.B.C., Incorporated
One Main Street, U.S.A.
(555) 555-5555

Dear   :

You might remember that I wrote you about three weeks ago concerning a background interview for a story on the opening of our firm's new offices. Such an article would make an interesting feature for your business pages.

Since then I have tried without success to contact you on three occasions. Have you received my messages?

It might be better if you telephoned me instead. My office number is on the letterhead above, and my home number is 555-2032.

I should point out that since our last press release the firm has published another book, <u>Low-Profile Investing</u>, that is doing very well and is receiving very favorable reviews. We also are receiving favorable coverage from several television stations.

I will contact you again if we do not get in touch within the next few days.

Sincerely,

John Smith

John Smith

LETTER ASKING TO MAKE A SPEECH

One of the most powerful publicity tools you have is yourself. No one knows the business better than you, and how better to spread that knowledge than by making speeches. But no one will know that you are available for speech-making, unless you tell them. And, that's what this letter is for.

Tips on How to Customize Your Letter:

1. In the opening explain your qualifications and what you want to use them for.

2. Go into detail about your presentation, what it is about, how long it is, why you want to give it for this group, how they will benefit, etc.

3. As a business owner, your strongest asset is your experience, play up on it.

4. Talk about your track record and actually offer references if you feel it is necessary.

More Useful Paragraphs:

• Over the past 35 years, after owning 22 companies, I have found out the right and wrong ways to manage people.

• I would like the opportunity to express my thoughts and share my experiences with your organization some time this fall.

• My presentation is built around a slide show and encompasses both the traditional management styles and those of the Japanese business. But the conclusion is based on my observations and mostly on my own experience managing people. What to do and when to do it are demonstrated. I usually close my presentation with a question - and - answer period.

• I have a script, a video tape, and a list of past organizations which have heard my presentation. If you are interested, I would be more than happy to forward this material to you.

• Thank you for your consideration. I certainly hope we can get together on this project as I feel we both could benefit greatly.

A.B.C., Incorporated
One Main Street, U.S.A.
(555) 555-5555

Dear Program Chairman:

I believe I have developed a presentation that would be suitable for an EA seminar and would like to know if the presentation could be arranged. During my three years in the Entrepreneurs Association, I have attended many of our conventions and seminars.

My topic is "How To Hire Your First Employee." I have spoken on this subject to several local groups, and it has been well received. Prior talks have run 1 1/2 hours, including questions and answers, but can be modified to 45 minutes if necessary. Most entrepreneurs have faced the same problem I did. Organizations such as the EA tell us how to start a small business and how to develop personnel policies, but nobody tells us how to go from having no employees to having ten.

I made several mistakes during this process myself and believe I can tell others how to avoid making these and other mistakes.

If you are interested, I can send a tape of one of the earlier presentations. Then we can begin discussing the details of the presentation for the EA.

This talk has been well received by other groups, and I believe the EA members would find it useful as well.

Sincerely,

John Smith

John Smith

*Letter asking to make
a speech*

CHAPTER 11

Building Personal and Community Goodwill

Ultimately business success depends on people—those who work for you and those you do business with. If you want to maximize your success, you need to pay attention to personal matters as well as to the dollars and cents.

The personal business letter and goodwill letters are similar. Their intent is the same—to generate allegiance by showing personal interest—but the events occasioning the letters are different. Goodwill letters are optional. You look for opportunities to send them. Many personal letters on the other hand, are obligatory, but still are crucially important to cementing relationships and building goodwill.

Personal letters usually express solicitude, congratulations or thanks related to nonbusiness events. They may be handwritten, typed on personal stationery, or on business letterhead. But they generally contain no reference to business. The personal letter should be short and informal. The degree of informality depends on your relationship with the reader. You want a letter that is sincere and will be appreciated by the reader.

A *goodwill letter* is a unique combination of a sales letter and a personal letter. Goodwill letters generally express sentiments such as congratulations or good luck; these letters also should be concise, simple and sincere.

Many businesses overlook the tremendous sales potential of goodwill letters. Since the letters usually express personal sentiments, the business potential is not immediately apparent. But the goodwill letter keeps a firm in the customer's mind and builds a positive image for the firm. Over the long term this helps the business by generating referrals and putting the company first in the customer's mind. The goodwill letter produces sales by telling people that you give personal attention to customers.

Writing the goodwill letter is fairly easy. The most important and difficult part of the process is selecting the events which warrant letters. You should decide in advance which events should cause you to send a goodwill letter, then develop a bank of letters for those occasions. You must develop a system for monitoring the events, adapting the form letters to individual situations, and mailing the letters. Remember that a goodwill letter is effective only if the recipient believes it is sincere. Therefore, the letter must be timely and personal.

The more common occasions for sending goodwill letters are:

- birthdays
- holidays (Christmas cards are a form of goodwill letter)
- anniversaries (either personal or business)
- large orders
- prompt payment record
- becoming a new customer
- opening of a new office or branch
- introduction of a new product
- personnel changes
- moving into the neighborhood
- successfully concluding a deal together

There probably are other events that are unique to your area, industry or customers. You should try to send at least one letter a year to each customer.

Sometimes a sales pitch or reference to business is appropriate in a goodwill letter. But the point of a goodwill letter is to show you care about the recipient personally, and this objective might be defeated by including a direct sales pitch. The writer must carefully consider whether or not a discussion of his firm is appropriate for the letter he is writing.

WELCOME LETTER TO NEW RESIDENTS

Individuals and/or families that move into your area, as well as new businesses are potential new customers. It's wise to get off to a good, solid start with the people and business by welcoming them to the area.

Tips on How to Customize Your Letter:

1. Be warm and friendly in your letter.

2. Let the reader feel truly welcome to this new place.

3. Of course, include a mild sales pitch on your company.

4. Make a sincere effort and gesture to help the new resident become acclimated.

Optional Paragraphs and Phrases:

- Welcome to Wilmington! We are honored to have a new gourmet restaurant in our midst.

- We just found out you have relocated to our fair city. Welcome! And, as soon as you have the time, stop by and visit.

- One of the frustrating parts of moving to a new area is finding out who's who and what's what. Let me take this opportunity to introduce our organization and tell you a little about us.

- Please accept this bound history of the area as our gift. It should help you understand what has made our city what it is today.

- Again, welcome neighbor. We are so glad to have you nearby.

- You've made a great choice. We think _____ is one of the best places in the country.

- It's my pleasure to welcome you to _____ . We're going to do everything we can to see that you enjoy living here.

- As part of our welcome to new residents, we offer a 15% discount on your first purchase up to $100 from our store. Come in to browse around and don't forget to bring the enclosed coupon.

- Come in and say hello. We're glad to have you as a neighbor and believe we have a lot to offer you.

- As a new resident, you are eligible for special consideration when applying for an ABC charge account. This account offers several features that should interest you.

- We want you to know us better. Many of your neighbors consider us to be a valuable part of the community, and we think you'll come to agree with them.

A.B.C., Incorporated
One Main Street, U.S.A.
(555) 555-5555

Dear   :

   We are glad we have the opportunity to welcome you to
         . Over the last ten years we have watched this area
grow and prosper, and it is always nice to learn that another
person has been attracted here.

   One of the difficulties with moving into a new area is
finding a good auto mechanic. Many new and longtime residents
come to our firm when their cars need work. Our staff of
certified mechanics provides fast, efficient service on most
foreign and domestic cars.

   Our rates are competitive with any auto shop in the area,
and we guarantee our service for 30 days. If you think we have
not repaired your car properly, bring it back within 30 days, and
we will do it right--at no charge.

   To help you get adjusted to your new community, we have
enclosed a printed card of important local telephone numbers to
place next to your phone. We are sure you will enjoy living
here, and we wish you the best.

                              Sincerely,

                              John Smith

                              John Smith

THANKING A NEW CUSTOMER

The small amount of time it will take you to write a thank you letter to a new customer may be redeemed many times over when the customer becomes a regular as a result of your thoughtfulness. Not only that, but that same customer will pass the word to all of his or her friends, relatives, and associates that you are a pleasure to work with and they must go to you. See what just one little letter can do!

Tips on How to Customize Your Letter:

1. First off, sincerely thank the customer for his or her valuable patronage.

2. Explain what customer loyalty means to you and how much you enjoy pleasing your customers.

3. Offer ongoing availability for questions, complaints or suggestions.

Optional Paragraphs and Phrases:

• One of the things I enjoy most about owning my own business is dealing with customers like you.

• Thank you so much for your order. We are truly pleased you have chosen to do business with us.

• Please understand that we will do everything in our power to make sure you are satisfied enough with our products and service to become a regular customer.

• Time does not allow me to speak to our customers very often when they are in the store. Please feel free, however, to contact me at any time for any service I can help you with.

• Again, thank you so much for your order. We hope to see you again very soon.

• Thanks for patronizing our firm. You've joined a growing list of businesses who appreciate an insurance agency that is concerned about something other than its commissions.

• One of the easiest parts of my jobs is welcoming a new customer. In the past few years I've been spending more and more time welcoming customers, so we must be doing something right.

• Customers are too important to lose, and I want you to understand from the start that I don't ever want to lose you. If you are ever less than totally satisfied, please give me an opportunity to make things right.

• Whenever we undertake to do something for you, we will do our utmost to satisfy you. We stand behind everything we do and will abide by every estimate we make.

A.B.C., Incorporated
One Main Street, U.S.A.
(555) 555-5555

Dear   :

    It is so gratifying to learn that we have attracted you as a new customer. I mean it sincerely when I say, "Thank you for your patronage."

    In fact, the only thing that could be more pleasing than your new business would be to get your repeat orders. I would like you to be a satisfied long-time customer so much that I will do everything I can to see that you are pleased. Once your name is on our client list, I want it to stay there.

    One of my highest priorities is to establish a long-term business relationship between our companies, so call me personally if there is anything I might be able to do to help you.

              Sincerely,

              John Smith

              John Smith

Thanking a new customer

HOLIDAY GREETINGS

Holidays are always a good time to pass along a little goodwill to your customers. They are a good time to let your customers hear from you and let them know that you are thinking of them.

Tips on How to Customize Your Letters:

1. You can get preprinted cards for various holidays, especially Christmas. While these are nice, you can enhance relations further with a personal touch so many people are looking for.

2. Give the holiday salutation.

3. Let customers know you want to celebrate the holiday with them.

4. Offer hope and positive thoughts for the time to come after the holiday.

Optional Paragraphs and Phrases:

● Happy President's Day!

● We know a lot of people think of today as a day for sales. We would like to take the time today to thank you for your patronage.

● Holidays would never be the same without people you care about to think of. And we do care about you!

● Have a wonderful holiday and may the rest of this year and all of next be the most wonderful time you've experienced.

● Please accept our fondest wishes for the New Year.

● Thank you for all you've done for us over the past year.

● We are happy this year has brought our association with you.

● Happy Easter. We hope the spring season with its renewal of life will give you pleasure.

A.B.C., Incorporated
One Main Street, U.S.A.
(555) 555-5555

Happy New Year!

    Soon we will be ringing in the new year. And as we look
back on this past year, we are extremely grateful for your
confidence in us and consider it one of the things we have to be
thankful for.

    We send you our sincerest and warmest wishes for a new year
filled with health, happiness and prosperity.

            Sincerely,

            John Smith

Holiday greeting — customer oriented

A.B.C., Incorporated
One Main Street, U.S.A.
(555) 555-5555

Dear   :

   As much as I would like to, I cannot find a better way to
say "Merry Christmas." The more I try, the more I realize that
no other phrase makes such a strong expression of joy, fellow-
ship, love and hope. I think I will stop trying to find a
replacement.

   So, Merry Christmas to you, and all the good things that go
with that thought.

   Since I cannot see you in person to deliver the message,
this letter will have to do. May the next year be even better
than the last.

                    Sincerely,

                    John Smith

                    John Smith

Holiday greeting — general

CONGRATULATORY

Everyone appreciates congratulations when they've done something they are especially proud of. Take the time to congratulate your colleagues, associates, employees, and friends on their promotions, grand openings, graduations, etc.

Tips on How to Customize Your Letters:

1. Send your congratulations as close to the event as possible.

2. Use an informal, conversational tone.

3. Be enthusiastic. Show your pride; don't make it sound like an obligation.

4. As usual, be brief.

Optional Paragraphs and Phrases:

- I am so glad I stayed up last night to watch the election returns. Congratulations on your victory! A better person could not have won.

- We were delighted to hear about your son graduating magna cum laude from Harvard. How proud you must be!

- Congratulations on becoming a grandmother!

- Although I'm not pleased with the competition you provide, I am thrilled about your decision to go into business. Your ability and quality of work will certainly keep me on my toes!

- Again, accept our most heartfelt congratulations. We are positively thrilled for you.

- Congratulations and best wishes.

- Your recent promotion must be very satisfying. I know you worked hard for it.

- Let me offer you my congratulations and best wishes. News of your recent award just reached me.

- You must be pleased at your colleague's election to the presidency of the bar association. Please pass along my congratulations.

A.B.C., Incorporated
One Main Street, U.S.A.
(555) 555-5555

Dear   :

    I just read about your recent promotion! I cannot say it was a surprise.

    The work we have done together over the last few years has been a real pleasure, and this is a business where usually the only pleasure comes from closing a deal. Your professionalism and creativity even made handling those inevitable last-minute changes and problems much less of an ordeal than they usually are.

    I gather from your job title that we still will have opportunities to work together. I hope we can continue these mutually profitable endeavors.

                  Sincerely,

                  John Smith

Letter of congratulations — goodwill

A.B.C., Incorporated
One Main Street, U.S.A.
(555) 555-5555

Dear   :

    We heard about your grand opening and are glad to welcome
you to the   business community. There is no greater
personal accomplishment than operating a business.

    We would like to help you in any way we can. As you might
know, we are the area's leading office supply outlet. Because of
our high volume, we can offer the most competitive prices available. Come visit our main sales center or ask for a catalog when
things get less hectic.

    Again, we offer our sincerest congratulations and best
wishes on your new venture.

                Sincerely,

                John Smith

                John Smith

Letter of congratulations — personal

LETTER TO LONG-TERM CUSTOMER

Just as important as new customers are to your business, long standing, regular customers are its mainstay. Every once in a while it is nice to let them know how much you appreciate them and their business.

Tips on How to Customize Your Letter:

1. Specify the amount of time you have been associated with the customer.

2. Express your gratitude for their allegiance and faith deeply and honestly.

3. Let the reader know you are willing to return the loyalty in any way you can.

Optional Paragraphs and Phrases:

• The past five years have been tremendous. One of the major reasons is having you as a customer.

• Your loyalty and patronage over the past years have literally allowed this company to grow.

• I find it difficult to express in words how much I appreciate having you as a customer and loyal business associate.

• Times over the past twenty-five years have not always been easy, but you have stood by us through thick and thin. For that we are eternally grateful.

• I wish I could figure out just how many of our present clients have come to us because of your referrals. I would guess over 50%. Thank you from the bottom of my heart for that kind of support.

• I realize that the words "thank you" are hardly enough to express my gratitude to you. Please let me know if there is anything I can do for you in the future to help to return the kind of backing I have received from you.

• Writing this letter is one of the greatest pleasures I've had. You have been one of our customers for five years this month.

• Anniversaries are happy occasions, and this one is a particularly happy event for us.

• I believe that a business relationship of this length is no accident. We must be doing something right, and we'll be doing our best to continue it.

• You should know by now that you are a preferred customer. We want you to continue to buy from us, and we will exert ourselves to retain your confidence and trust.

A.B.C., Incorporated
One Main Street, U.S.A.
(555) 555-5555

Dear   :

    A decade is a long time. But that is how long I have been able to count on you as a customer.

    I wanted you to know how much I appreciate the faith and cooperation you have shown in the company. I remember times when money was tight and you paid more quickly than you had to, or when our business was growing faster than production could handle it - and you did not complain about late shipments. I appreciate all this very much.

    Over the years I hope we have been able to return the favors a few times. Whether or not we have, we will do so as often as possible in the future. You are the kind of customer we want to keep.

                    Sincerely,

                    John Smith

                    John Smith

Letter to long-term customer

LETTER COMPLIMENTING A SUPPLIER

A good word about a job well done always motivates someone to continue to do good or even better work for the person who passed along the compliment. It is especially important to let suppliers and vendors know when they've done well. So often they hear complaints, that if you compliment them, you are bound to stand out in their favor for the next job you want done or order you want delivered.

Tips on How to Customize Your Letter:

1. As with any thank you or complimentary letter, be sincere.

2. Unless you are sending a general "you've been a wonderful supplier" letter, try to be specific about the incident you are referring to.

3. Allow the letter to take on a personal, friendly tone; don't make it an obligation.

Optional Paragraphs and Phrases:

• The turnaround time we required for our last book printing was almost asking the impossible. It's incredible that your firm managed to produce the books on schedule.

• You have always provided us with good service, but the last job you completed for us was totally outstanding.

• A large part of what makes our business successful is suppliers like yourself who we can trust and depend on totally.

• There is positively no way we could have met our deadline, if you hadn't burned the midnight oil to meet yours. Thank you.

• You've shown that your firm really wants our business. Time and again you've come through under unreasonable conditions.

• Too many businesses don't realize that the intangible factors count just as much as price. Quality, promptness, and courtesy all are important to us, and they obviously are important to you.

• I know things are hectic right now, but the outstanding service you've provided us requires that I take time out to compliment you.

• The creativity and initiative of your staff never ceases to amaze me, and this week you've done it again. Several other companies told us that what we wanted was impossible; they wouldn't even consider it. But you came through with a better job than we had hoped for.

A.B.C., Incorporated
One Main Street, U.S.A.
(555) 555-5555

Dear   :

    For the past year you have rendered invaluable assistance to our firm, and I do not want that assistance to be overlooked.

    You have done more than provide us with the products we need at fair prices. We have received goods promptly despite short notice and been granted generous repayment terms that some of your competitors refused us. We appreciate your confidence in our firm and believe it has been instrumental in our success over the last year.

    I hope that over the coming year we will be able to return some of the courtesies you have shown us. I look forward to a relationship that continues to build the profitability of both our companies.

                      Sincerely,

                      John Smith

Letter complimenting a supplier

THANK YOU LETTER FOR A SPECIAL FAVOR
AND A GENERAL THANK YOU

Special favors are special because they require someone to go that extra mile for you. They deserve special recognition and thanks.

Tips on How to Customize Your Letter:

1. Reiterate the favor.

2. Give sincere thanks.

3. Offer to reciprocate at any time in the future.

Optional Paragraphs and Phrases:

• Thank you so much for the extra research you did for me. It made my job in completing the article so much more thorough and easier. How would I ever have met my deadline, if you hadn't typed the manuscript in record time? I wouldn't have, that's all! I realize how much overtime you had to put in and I appreciate it more than you can imagine.

• Words cannot explain the gratitude I feel for the support you gave me when my father was so ill. I truly don't think I could have made it through that trying time without you.

• You may not think that listening to my trials and tribulations is any big deal, but it is. And for your patience and understanding, I am eternally grateful

• Thank you again for your help. If I can do the same for you at any time, please be sure to tell me.

• I hope you understand how much I appreciate what you have done for me and for the company. I intend to return the favor as soon as I possibly can.

A.B.C., Incorporated
One Main Street, U.S.A.
(555) 555-5555

Dear   :

As you know, our company just went through an especially trying period. You know about this because you were instrumental in a successful resolution of our problems.

We cannot tell you how much we appreciate your efforts in this matter. The best I can offer is this sincere expression of profound gratitude. Without the extraordinary efforts of you and a few others, this period would have ended very unpleasantly.

Again, I offer our heartfelt thanks and a pledge to return the favor should you ever need it.

Cordially,

John Smith

John Smith

Thank you letter for a special favor

A.B.C., Incorporated
One Main Street, U.S.A.
(555) 555-5555

Dear   :

    I cannot tell you how much I appreciated your letter.

    Though I am out of the hospital and getting around, it will be several more weeks before I am strong enough to put in full days at the office. I am, however, working out of the house and keeping a close tab on your account. You can be sure that I am doing all I can to keep our best customers, such as you, satisfied.

    Thank you again for your letter. I hope to be back on the job soon.

               Sincerely,

               John Smith

               John Smith

SYMPATHY LETTERS

Expressing your sympathy to someone who has lost a loved one or who is suffering from an ailment or accident can be very difficult. Worse yet, the more you labor over this kind of letter, the more insincere it sounds. The best way to express your sympathy is to simply write what you feel. Don't worry about the words, your honest feelings and wishes will make them come out just right.

Tips on How to Customize Your Letters:

1. Focus on your reader. Don't discuss anything about yourself except how you feel for the reader

2. Try to avoid a stiff, formal tone.

3. Be as brief as you can while adequately expressing your thoughts.

4. Most important, be honest and sincere.

Optional Paragraphs and Phrases:

• I am sorry to hear about the tragedy of fire that has befallen you and your family. To say we are shocked would be an understatement.

• Please let us know if there is anything at all that we can do to help.

• I am sincere in my offer to have you and your family stay at my house until some order returns to your lives.

• We were so sorry to hear about the death of _____ . Over the years, his advice had become invaluable to the operation of our company. Both personally and professionally he will be dearly missed.

• I heard late last night about your accident over the weekend. I was relieved to hear that you weren't injured too extensively. However, any injury or inconvenience at the hands of a drunken driver is inexcusable and unforgivable. Please know that we are doing all we can to get these type of people off the roads.

• Please let me know how I can be of help to you in this time of grief.

• Always know I am here for anything you may need, even just to talk.

• I know that a stay in the hospital is always frustrating, and I wish there was something I could do to help.

• You have many friends and associates here at ABC, and we want you back working with us.

• We hope that your stay in the hospital will be short and your recovery will be rapid. We want you back at work.

• We were all shocked to hear the tragic news of _____ 's death. Please add our sympathy and condolences to the many we're sure you've already received.

• The tragic news saddened all of us here. _____ was a fine businessman and friend. We will miss him both personally and as a business associate.

A.B.C., Incorporated
One Main Street, U.S.A.
(555) 555-5555

Dear   :

    We were shocked to hear of your partner's sudden death. On behalf of all of us here, I offer our sincerest condolences.

    Jim was one of the first people I met after starting my own business, and we shared a lot of cherished memories together. Jim always did his best for the customer. Several times he helped us through tough periods. We will miss him.

    I know Jim will be difficult to replace. No doubt the next few months will be trying for you. We plan to offer you all the assistance Jim gave us during our long association. Just call whenever you need something.

                Sincerely,

                John Smith

                John Smith

Letter of sympathy — death

A.B.C., Incorporated
One Main Street, U.S.A.
(555) 555-5555

Dear   :

  I learned this morning that you have been in the hospital
for two weeks. It was good to hear that your operation was
successful and that you are beginning to feel like your old self.

  If there is anything I can do to help, please call. I have
always enjoyed working with you and look forward to doing so
again soon.

       Sincerely,

       John Smith

       John Smith

Letter of sympathy — hospital stay

A.B.C., Incorporated
One Main Street, U.S.A.
(555) 555-5555

Dear   :

    I was very distressed to read about the tragedy at your plant. It must be very difficult to see a fine facility such as yours destroyed by fire. I am sure, however, that you have the courage and resourcefulness to bounce back.

    We are very interested in doing whatever we can to help you. We have had a long, mutually cooperative relationship, and our firm will do all it can to continue this relationship.

           Sincerely,

           John Smith

Letter of sympathy — fire

HOSPITALITY LETTER

An effective goodwill builder is a quick thank you to someone who has offered you hospitality, be it a business associate, vendor, relative, or friend. The following example will offer you a way to accomplish this without taking a lot of time.

Tips on How to Customize Your Letter:

1. Be grateful but don't go overboard.

2. Be brief and to the point.

3. Specify what benefit you received from the visit.

4. Express recognition for any behavior that was particularly hospitable, such as lunch, car at the airport, tour of the plant, etc.

Optional Paragraphs and Phrases:

• I really appreciated being shown around your premises the other day. The visit was a real learning experience.

• It was kind of you to take us to lunch last week to discuss your recent proposal. We really appreciated the gesture.

• The hospitality you showed us on our visit last week was impressive. I think it helped to advance our business discussions and produced a better working relationship.

• Most people consider a business lunch to be an obligation. But you obviously treated the occasion as a real opportunity to entertain, and I want you to know that your efforts are appreciated.

A.B.C., Incorporated
One Main Street, U.S.A.
(555) 555-5555

Dear   :

    I want to thank you for the lunch and presentation you arranged for us yesterday. My colleagues and I believe the discussions resulted in a good deal of progress in our contract negotiations.

    The trouble you went to in planning our visit probably allowed us to complete our work in a fraction of the time we anticipated.

    As we decided yesterday, we will be submitting our next proposal to you within two weeks. Thanks so much for the great hospitality and effective presentation.

          Sincerely,

          John Smith

          John Smith

Hospitality letter

APOLOGIES

When an error is made, one way to redeem yourself and recreate goodwill is to write a quick note apologizing for the situation. As shown in the following examples, the letter can include a corrective action or not, depending on the appropriateness of the situation.

Tips on How to Customize Your Letter:

1. Admit that you were wrong, but don't chastise yourself.
2. Make the apology in a brief, straightforward manner.
3. Be warm and friendly.

Optional Paragraphs and Phrases:

- Please accept my apology for not being able to attend the shareholder's meeting last week.

- On behalf of the company, I want to apologize for the lack of communication that has caused such a bad situation.

- I was totally embarrassed this morning when I saw the package that was to be sent by express mail to you yesterday. Needless to say, I have delivered it to the post office myself first thing this morning.

- I am sorry to have inadvertently left out the enclosures I mentioned in my letter of _____ . They are being sent to you under separate cover today.

- I'm sorry about having to cancel our appointment yesterday. You know that I wouldn't do this without good reason.

- I'm sorry I haven't gotten in touch with you before now. We've had several emergencies here, and I've been unable to keep my correspondence up to date.

- You've been a great help to me, and I feel really bad about not answering your letter before now. I was embarrassed when I found that your letter had been put on the bottom of the correspondence pile.

- There really is no excuse for a product being sent from here in the condition of the one you purchased. Despite the precautions we take, however, it happens once in a while.

- I regret the problems you encountered in our office last week. You certainly deserve more than a simple apology.

- This apology cannot make up for all the damage you've suffered, but I hope you will accept it.

A.B.C., Incorporated
One Main Street, U.S.A.
(555) 555-5555

Dear   :

    When I told you that our report would be complete by
March 15, this seemed like a reasonable deadline. Our study,
however, has revealed the project to be far more complicated than
either you or I imagined. We cannot do a quality job by our
original deadline.

    As we discussed on the phone several times recently, the
research is producing very favorable results. Your firm should
get several very profitable suggestions from this document,
making the additional wait worthwhile.

    We will definitely have the report completed and in your
hands no later than April 30.

                  Sincerely,

                  John Smith

Letter of apology

A.B.C., Incorporated
One Main Street, U.S.A.
(555) 555-5555

Dear   :

    Thank you for your letter telling me about the unsatis-
factory service you received last week.

    It is unfortunate, but occasionally a mistake is made
despite how careful or well trained the personnel are. After
reviewing your letter and talking with the crew assigned to the
job, I have concluded that this is what happened in your case.
We deeply regret this mistake.

    I hope you will give us another try - at no additional
charge to you. If you prefer to go with another firm, we
understand and will mark your account "paid in full."

        Sincerely,

        John Smith

        John Smith

Letter apologizing and making an adjustment

RECOMMENDATION LETTER

As we mentioned in Chapter 1, recommendations should not be made randomly. If you honestly feel someone, employee, vendor, or colleague has done an outstanding job, write them a recommendation. This letter may be written whether it is solicited or not.

Tips on How to Customize Your Letter:

1. Be enthusiastic.

2. Give the reader the appropriate facts to work with.

3. Adopt a personal tone.

Optional Paragraphs and Phrases:

• I am pleased to offer a recommendation for _____, even though I have not been solicited to do so. I felt it necessary to put into writing what an outstanding job _____ has done on the construction of our home.

• I have known _____ for the past decade, and though it is not my normal policy to do so, I recommend him highly for any position he may seek.

• Dr. Mutt's Veterinary Services has long been taking care of the large stock animals on my farm. I highly recommend that anyone with animals of any type seek the services of Dr. Mutt's.

• As you know, I don't give unqualified recommendations to many people, but I might make an exception in _____'s case.

• _____ and I have been closely associated for four years. She's shown herself capable of handling the pressure-cooker environment that is so prevalent in this industry.

• _____ is not only good at his job but also is a great morale booster around the office. His sense of humor and pleasant personality keep the office atmosphere harmonious and productive.

A.B.C., Incorporated
One Main Street, U.S.A.
(555) 555-5555

Dear   :

    I would like to tell you more about Tom Snow, the real estate broker I mentioned at lunch yesterday.

    Over the last five years, Tom has represented me in a number of real estate deals. As you know, I have been involved in real estate for many years and have had numerous problems with brokers. But Tom has proven to be the ideal broker. In the last three years I have not used any other broker and have been more satisfied with the results than I have been in years.

    Tom is one of those rare brokers who understands that his bottom line improves only if his principal's bottom line improves. I am sure you can appreciate how he is different from the typical broker.

    I can unhesitatingly recommend Tom Snow for any real estate deal you have in the works.

                Sincerely,

                John Smith

                John Smith

Recommendation letter

CIVIC PROJECT INVITATION

When inviting someone to join a civic or charitable project or organization, you need to be convincing. You are essentially asking someone to take their valuable time to work on a non-money-making project. This is a hard sell job!

Tips on How to Customize Your Letters:

1. Be direct and polite in tone.

2. For the invitation, go back to your sales letter mode. Compliment the person being invited and explain how this can enhance the project and how the project can be good for them.

3. Close the invitation with the assumption that the person will accept.

Optional Paragraphs and Phrases:

• I know you're busy. All successful businessmen are. But I think you recognize that businessmen must be involved in community activities these days.

• Though we are a nonprofit organization, we need the decision-making abilities of experienced businessmen. We have the same problems regarding cost cutting, personnel, and public acceptance that most businesses have.

• We have a full-time staff to handle the day-to-day affairs. We need your expertise for policy decisions.

• It's time for our annual fund-raising drive, and we've found that no one can raise funds better than a prominent businessman. Your stature in the community will do wonders for this worthwhile cause.

A.B.C., Incorporated
One Main Street, U.S.A.
(555) 555-5555

Dear   :

I know that you appreciate the importance of the Fairfax
County Planning Authority to the health and welfare of our
community. The Authority allows our county to grow without
producing the unseemly effects of growth found in so many other
localities.

To do its job effectively, the Authority depends on an
outside board of advisors to suggest changes in the Master Plan
and comment on specific proposals before the Authority. The
board is composed of outstanding citizens and business leaders
such as you, those who have demonstrated an ability to balance
business and nonbusiness considerations.

Accordingly, the Authority invites you to join its board of
advisors. This is a crucial time for the county, and we need the
advice of knowledgeable, thoughtful people like you. This is a
rare opportunity to have a long-term impact on your community.

Please call me at the number above to let me know your
decision. We are planning a welcome luncheon for our new board
members on August 25. You might want to reserve that date on
your calendar now.

Sincerely,

John Smith

John Smith

Civic project invitation

DECLINING CIVIC PROJECT INVITATION

When you need to decline an invitation, you do need to be polite and gracious, but be firm as well. Let the people inviting you know that, without a doubt, you simply haven't the time to spare, although you are honored with the invitation.

Tips on How to Customize Your Letter:

1. Be as firm as you can be while maintaining a tone of gratitude for the invitation.

2. Emphasize how honored you are and how you value the worth of the project. Then explain that you haven't the time necessary to give proper attention to such a project.

3. Close the declination with an offer to help in the future.

Optional Paragraphs and Phrases:

• This invitation is one of the highest compliments I have received. I have great respect for your organization.

• Our firm is just hitting a strong growth phase, and I must devote more than full time to the business in order to seize this opportunity.

• This year I have committed myself to more community activities than I can handle. It is just impossible for me to accept any more responsibility this year.

• Several of my commitments are temporary appointments that will expire within the next 12 months. If you are still interested, I would be glad to serve at that time.

A.B.C., Incorporated
One Main Street, U.S.A.
(555) 555-5555

Dear   :

Thank you for the invitation to join the board of advisors of the Authority. I realize the importance of the job and the immense compliment of being offered this position.

Because I realize the importance of this job, I must decline the invitation. Regrettably, I have made several long-term commitments that probably will absorb all of my free time for the foreseeable future. I cannot devote enough time to the board to do the job properly.

Thank you again for the invitation, and I hope you will consider me again in the future.

Sincerely,

John Smith

John Smith

Letter declining a civic invitation

LETTER OF INTRODUCTION

There are two ways to present a letter of introduction. It can be presented in person almost as a calling card, or it can be mailed to the addressee. Either way, the letter should be brief, informative, and courteous.

Tips on How to Customize Your Letter:

1. State the reason for the introduction, the name of the person being introduced, and his or her commendations in the first half of the letter.

2. Add some personal information to make the letter and the meeting more friendly.

3. Arrange a meeting and/or express your confidence in the person to close.

Optional Paragraphs and Phrases:

• I just heard that a longtime friend of mine, _____ , has opened his own financial planning practice in your area. Mark has given me successful financial advice for years, and I think you would benefit from consulting with him.

• There really isn't anyone I can recommend more highly than _____ . You know that I don't usually toss superlatives about casually.

• _____ believes in putting service first. I've never heard of him turning down any request that seemed probable. You'll find that his enthusiasm and optimism is overwhelming.

• I know you've had problems getting the right kind of service, and I believe _____ can solve most of your problems. He's always served me well.

A.B.C., Incorporated
One Main Street, U.S.A.
(555) 555-5555

Dear   :

    I would like to introduce you to a long-time colleague of mine, Gary C. Byler.

    Gary, whom I think I have mentioned to you before, is a first-rate computer consultant and programmer. He has done some very valuable work for me in the past, and I thought you could benefit from his services.

    Since Gary will be on an extended trip in the northeast region in a few months, you can expect him to call you and ask for an appointment. Based on past discussions you and I have had on computers, I think you could profit from meeting Gary.

          Sincerely,

          John Smith

          John Smith

Letter of introduction

PRESENTING, ACCEPTING AND DECLINING AN INFORMAL INVITATION

When making an informal invitation your number one thought should be extending goodwill.

When accepting such an invitation, be straightforward. This is an easy task, it is pleasurable and no excuses need to be made.

When declining an invitation, be polite and at all costs avoid offending the reader.

Tips on How to Customize Your Letters:

1. For extending an invitation: be gracious and friendly, and be sure to include all pertinent information about the event.

2. Formal invitations are usually pre-printed on card stock and enclosed in lined envelopes.

3. For declining an invitation: be prompt with your reply, even though it is unpleasant don't put it off; be tactful but honest about why you can't attend.

Optional Paragraphs and Phrases:

FOR INVITATIONS

• I understand that you are going to be in New Orleans in two weeks. By coincidence, I'll be there at the same time. Perhaps we could get together if there's time in your schedule.

• Things are going to be hectic at the national convention in two months. That's why I'm writing you early to ask if we could schedule some time together. I think we would both benefit tremendously.

• I always benefit from meetings with you, and I hope you receive enough benefit to schedule another meeting.

FOR ACCEPTING AN INVITATION

• I benefitted tremendously from our past meetings, and I'd be glad to schedule another with you.

• I was hoping that you could find time for me at the convention. My schedule is very flexible at this point, and I'd be happy to reserve some time to spend with you.

• Your suggestion is an excellent one. I'd be glad to meet you at the hospitality reception at 7:00 p.m.

• Thanks for thinking of me and offering to include me in your plans.

FOR DECLINING AN INVITATION

- Unfortunately, I will be attending only a part of the convention, and my schedule is so unsettled at this point that I cannot make any commitments.

- I'd really like to meet with you in New Orleans, but my itinerary simply doesn't leave any room for even a brief meeting.

- Regretfully I must decline your invitation for a meeting. I do appreciate the invitation and hope we can get together sometime.

- I've tried working with my schedule, but there is no alternative but to decline this opportunity to meet with you.

A.B.C., Incorporated
One Main Street, U.S.A.
(555) 555-5555

Dear   :

On Friday, June 12, ABC Company will be holding an open
house at its new offices. We would like you, one of our valued
customers, to attend.

The open house will begin at the address on this letterhead
with a ribbon-cutting ceremony at 5:30 and continue with tours of
the new offices accompanied by refreshments and a buffet.

Please let me know if you plan to attend. I would very much
like you to come and help us mark this milestone in our firm's
growth.

Sincerely,

John Smith

John Smith

Informal invitation

A.B.C., Incorporated
One Main Street, U.S.A.
(555) 555-5555

You are cordially invited to attend the Grand Opening of ABC, Inc.'s, new facilities.

The ceremony will take place on the premises of 100 Main Street, USA, and will begin at 2 p.m. on Thursday, April 30, 1989.

An open bar and refreshments will be provided.

R.S.V.P.--Regrets Only--555/555-5555.

Formal invitation

A.B.C., Incorporated
One Main Street, U.S.A.
(555) 555-5555

Dear   :

    I am glad to accept the invitation to attend your open house. I look forward to meeting with you in this informal environment.

    Watching and participating in ABC's growth has brought a great deal of pleasure to all of us here. I am sure this is just one of many milestones to come.

    Thanks for the invitation, and I will be sure to work it into my schedule.

            Sincerely,

            John Smith

            John Smith

Accepting an invitation

A.B.C., Incorporated
One Main Street, U.S.A.
(555) 555-5555

Dear   :

    I appreciate the invitation to your open house on June 12. As much as I would like to be there, however, my schedule takes me out of town for that entire week.

    This is certainly a milestone in ABC's development, and I look forward to many more. I will do my best to work in a visit to your new offices sometime in the near future, perhaps at a time when we can have lunch together.

    Thank you for your invitation and congratulations on this achievement.

                      Sincerely,

                      John Smith

                      John Smith

Declining an invitation

CHAPTER
12
Dealing with Suppliers

Relations with suppliers are a key part of doing business successfully for most companies. Carefully written communications are required in: getting quotes on prices and terms, negotiating contracts, confirming terms and rejecting or accepting proposals.

Many letters to suppliers amount to binding legal contracts. Unclear or incomplete communication can result in misquotes, wasted energy on both ends, frustrations, or even lawsuits.

None of this solidifies working relationships, so the importance of tact in the communication is also a strong element. Get the supplier working with you, not for you. Avoid alienating the supplier by wielding your purchasing power unnecessarily. You want to communicate to the supplier your needs in terms of product and service in a way that will generate the best product and service at a good price.

Letters to suppliers are more important than many business executives realize. The more effective letters are explicit, accurate, thorough, persuasive, and tactful. And, letters to suppliers must be effective for any business's success.

LETTER REQUESTING INFORMATION FROM A SUPPLIER

This letter should be as specific and clearly documented as possible to avoid a lot of misunderstanding, misconceptions, and wasted time. Let suppliers know right away what you are looking for or what you want from them, so they can provide you with information that exactly answers your needs.

Tips on How to Customize Your Letter:

1. Be exact, specific, clear and to-the-point, especially if you are contacting a new supplier.

2. Explain your situation so the supplier might be able to offer some useful information and ideas that you had not thought of.

3. Don't offer false hope of an order if you are just in the information collecting stage. Tell the supplier that after you have finished researching the market, you will be in contact.

Optional Paragraphs and Phrases:

- We are expanding our file of possible suppliers for office machinery.

- Please send us any information you have on your company, a catalogue of your products, and a price list.

- We are looking for a new method of binding our annual reports. So far we have thought of three-ring binders and spiral binding. Please give us information on these two methods, and any other suggestions you might have.

- To give you an idea of just who we are, our size, and what we do, I've enclosed our company's profile for your information.

- Thank you in advance for your time and effort. We will be in contact after our research is complete.

- We are expanding our product line and would like to include storm doors that qualify for the residential energy tax credit in our offerings. Please submit a price list of the items you have available.

- Can you offer a better employee health plan than the one we have? Enclosed is a copy of our current plan. Please submit your proposal as soon as possible.

A.B.C., Incorporated
One Main Street, U.S.A.
(555) 555-5555

Dear   :

    We are considering updating our office equipment to include
a word processing system. Before making a decision, we need to
know the prices, capabilities, maintenance records and expanda-
bility of the systems available. Some important considerations
to use are the quality of the documentation, the ease with which
a system can be used and the available training.

    We are a medium-sized service business and expect to
eventually acquire five word processors that are compatible with
each other. Additional functions, such as spreadsheet analysis
and budgeting, are less important to us right now. But a system
that could handle such tasks would be a plus.

    We thank you for your time and look forward to your reply.

            Sincerely,

            John Smith

Letter requesting information

REQUEST FOR BIDS FROM POSSIBLE SUPPLIERS

The best way to ensure clear, accurate information and communication, especially in business purchasing, is to send out a detailed Request For Bid or Request For Proposal from your prospective suppliers. Attached to such requests should be a cover letter with the specific conditions of the request detailed in it. Written requests for bids prevent harmful misunderstandings from happening later on in the project.

Tips on How to Customize Your Letter:

1. State the information you are requesting clearly and specifically.

2. Provide the supplier with all the necessary information so he or she can respond accurately to your request.

3. Be sure to assign a deadline to the request.

Optional Paragraphs and Phrases:

• Attached is a rendering of the new addition we are planning. Please quote in triplicate the cost of building such an addition completely, ready for occupancy.

• Please send us your prices for the attached list of items by next Tuesday, January 13, 19_____ .

• We are happy to open a bid to you for the new addition we are planning on having constructed next year.

• If you have any questions at all about this project, please contact _____ _____ right away to avoid any delays in receiving your quote.

• Be sure to enclose the cost of all plumbing, electrical work, lighting fixtures, finish carpentry, and final inside painting in your quote.

• Address your final bid to _____ no later than January 13, 1989.

• We are bidding for a general contract to rehabilitate 822 E. Baltimore St. The project will require extensive electrical wiring. If you are interested in being the electrical subcontractor, please submit a sealed bid to this office by December 1, 1985. All bids must conform to the enclosed summary and to the blueprints available for review at the offices of the ABC Company.

• ABC, Inc. currently has a housekeeping contract with an established firm. This contract expires in one month.

• Enclosed is a plan for landscaping the grounds surrounding the offices of ABC, Inc. Please submit your bid for performing this landscaping. We anticipate selecting a contractor by June 15. Therefore, all bids should be on my desk by June 1.

• We are refurbishing our offices. Please submit your quotations on any of the items described on the attached plan.

A.B.C., Incorporated
One Main Street, U.S.A.
(555) 555-5555

TO:

FROM:

SUBJECT: Request for bids for rehabilitating a building

DESCRIPTION: ABC, Incorporated, has acquired the building shell
located at 822 East Baltimore Street and desires to
rehabilitate the structure into an office building.
ABC plans to occupy the building on or before
June 1, 19 . Time is of the essence, and any
contract will contain penalties for missed deadlines. Blueprints for the office building are
available for study in the offices of ABC, Incorporated, during regular office hours. A summary of
the building plans and additional conditions is
attached.

DEADLINES: Sealed bids and accompanying technical proposals
that conform to the conditions of this letter, the
attached summary and the blueprints should be
submitted to ABC, Incorporated, by January 1, 19 .

PROPOSAL/BID REJECTION

Rejection is a necessary part of all business transactions. However, when rejecting a bid or proposal you want to be careful not to alienate the supplier permanently. Word your rejection in such a way that the facts are clear and the supplier does not take the rejection as a personal affront to his work and/or business. Also be certain to send a letter to all submitted bidders whether accepted or rejected. If you have rejected their bid, at least when they receive your letter they can close the file and move on to other projects.

Tips on How to Customize Your Letters:

1. Thank the supplier for the time and effort put into the bid or proposal.

2. Explain clearly why you are rejecting the bid or proposal.

3. Be sure wording and closing keep the channels open for possible future dealings with the supplier.

Optional Paragraphs and Phrases:

• The time and effort you put into your proposal of _____ is evident by its quality.

• We appreciate the time you took to give us such a detailed and accurate bid.

• Thank you for your proposal.

• We have carefully compared the responses we received to our request for bids, and unfortunately yours came in just too high for our budget this year.

• After deliberating over who to award the job to, we have decided to go with a firm a little closer geographically for the convenience.

• Again, thank you for submitting your proposal. We are very impressed with your firm and hope to do business with you on a future project.

• The high quality of your June 15 proposal indicates the time and effort you obviously put into it.

• We appreciate the comprehensive, well-documented proposal you submitted in response to our request for bids.

• Unfortunately, we cannot award you the contract because we need more liberal credit terms than you can offer.

• We have decided that our firm is not ready for this equipment just yet. When we have grown some more, we will again consider your firm.

• We believe your firm will have difficulty providing the quantity of material we need in a timely fashion.

• You will remain on our list of invitees, and we hope that in the future we will be able to contract with you.

• We continue to think highly of your firm and believe it is likely that we will be able to do business together in the future.

A.B.C., Incorporated
One Main Street, U.S.A.
(555) 555-5555

Dear   :

    Thank you for submitting a proposal for rehabilitating our
office building at 822 East Baltimore Street. We appreciate the
time and effort it took.

    We regret to inform you that another bidder is being awarded
the contract. This decision was based on several factors, but
price was the primary consideration.

    We will be sure to include you in any future invitations to
bid on our projects.

                    Sincerely,

                    John Smith

                    John Smith

Proposal rejection — general

A.B.C., Incorporated
One Main Street, U.S.A.
(555) 555-5555

Dear   :

    We have carefully evaluated the responses to our request for bids. After analysis and discussion of the unusually competitive responses, we have decided to award the contract to Long & Associates of Columbia, Maryland. While all of the proposals were of exceptionally high quality, we believed Long & Associates offered significant advantages in creativity and experience that are critical to our project.

    We were particularly impressed with the cost section of your generally excellent proposal. We appreciate the large amount of time and interest you put into it.

                Sincerely,

                John Smith

                John Smith

Proposal rejection — specific

AWARDING THE CONTRACT

This is a very happy letter for both client and supplier. But, in your relief over finally deciding on a supplier, don't forget to be thorough. The contract award or order should state clearly: the products or service, the date of delivery or completion, and all other specifics pertinent to the success of the project. Both the contract and the cover letter should be as exact and precise as humanly possible.

Tips on How to Customize Your Letters:

1. Provide description of the project and what you expect from the supplier and when.

2. Leave no room for misunderstandings.

3. Reemphasize any of the details that are especially important to the contract itself.

4. Leave room on the contract for the supplier to sign and have him or her return a signed copy. This way you both have attested to understanding what is written in the contract or order.

Optional Paragraphs and Phrases:

• We are pleased to enclose our purchase order (#2345) for the material discussed in your quote of _____ .

• Unless we hear otherwise from you, we will assume that the contents of the purchase order are in accordance with your understanding of our agreement.

• Please sign the enclosed two copies of the contract and return one to us and keep the other for your files.

• Please note the due date on our purchase order. It is crucial that we receive the material by that date. If we do not, the order will be considered null and void.

• Thank you for the quick way in which you responded to our bid request. We are looking forward to having our project completed with the same speed.

• We have been so pleased with your work over the past three years, that it gives us great pleasure to present the enclosed contract to you.

• One of the reasons we have awarded this large order to you is because of the excellent reputation you have in the industry. Be assured that if you provide us with similar service and product, we will be more than happy to spread that reputation even further.

• Enclosed is our purchase order conforming to the prices quoted in your estimate dated _____ .

• We are pleased with your quote of October 15. Please send us the materials exactly as stated in your quote.

• We are pleased to renew our housekeeping contract with you.

• Once again your bid was competitive with all other bids we received, and since we are satisfied with your past service, we decided to accept your bid.

A.B.C., Incorporated
One Main Street, U.S.A.
(555) 555-5555

Dear   :

It is our pleasure to award you the contract for rehabilitating our building at 822 East Baltimore Street on the strength
of your proposal dated

Our attorneys will shortly finish drafting the contract to
conform with our specifications and your bid. The contract
should be in your possession within a week. We would like to
have the contract signed within ten days after your receipt of it
and work begun immediately thereafter. You will receive our
initial payment when the contract is signed.

We are very impressed with your bid and with your firm's
reputation. We look forward to doing business with you.

Sincerely,

John Smith

John Smith

Contract award — contract to follow

A.B.C., Incorporated
One Main Street, U.S.A.
(555) 555-5555

Dear   :

   Your bid for landscaping the grounds surrounding the offices
of ABC, Incorporated, has been successful. We are pleased to
award the contract to you.

   We would like you to begin work immediately since the
grounds currently are unattractive. As stated in our request for
bids, work must be completed by

   Please sign each of the two copies of the contract that are
enclosed with this letter and return the original to us.

                              Sincerely,

                              John Smith

                              John Smith

Contract award — contract enclosed

COMPLAINT TO A SUPPLIER

Any time you have a problem with a supplier or contractor, you should contact them immediately in written form. Although a phone call may also be warranted, many situations require legal proof in the form of a written complaint. Should you decide to withhold payment until the complaint is answered, be sure to document the complaint in a timely manner. This can be an important source of legal protection if your business relationship sours.

Tips on How to Customize Your Letter:

1. Explain, in detail, just what your complaint is right at the beginning of the letter.

2. Don't attack the supplier, simply explain the situation and ask for a solution.

3. If you can think of any solutions yourself, offer them to the supplier.

4. Sign off on a friendly note. Try not to put the supplier on the defensive or the error may never be remedied.

Optional Paragraphs and Phrases:

• As you know, ABC, Inc. has been in business for over 40 years. We know your reputation for excellent workmanship, which is why I am notifying you of a problem we just experienced with one of your workers.

• We have enjoyed an excellent working relationship with you for many years now. This makes it even more of a concern to me when the price on your invoice is drastically higher than that you quoted to us, as represented in our purchase order 2345.

• The defects I have found are as follows:

• We are very concerned with the progress of the construction job you are completing for us. As we have explained in numerous past correspondence, the deadline we set is set in stone. So far you are no where near meeting that deadline. Please explain what you are planning on doing in order to meet the date we both agreed upon.

• I'm sure that this letter is all you needed to correct the situation. I look forward to receiving your confirmation that corrective measures have been taken by the end of next week.

• Your excellent reputation is an important asset. That is why we're surprised at the shipment of defective materials we just received.

• Customer service is a key to business success. Satisfying others is how we stay in business and grow. I know when our firm's performance falls short, I want to hear about it. You probably feel the same way. That's why I'm writing to you:

• Our contract is very specific about the delivery dates for your _____ . Prompt receipt of these materials is essential to the fulfillment of contracts we have with others.

A.B.C., Incorporated
One Main Street, U.S.A.
(555) 555-5555

Dear   :

    We are calling your attention to a serious problem in the performance of our contract for the rehabilitation of the building at 822 East Baltimore Street.

    As we have repeatedly told you over the telephone, progress on the building is well behind schedule. Despite our assertions that timely completion of the building is essential, nothing has been done to accelerate the speed of the work. In addition, the electrical work that has been completed does not comply with the contract specifications.

    We urge you to take all steps necessary to complete the project according to the contract terms. If we are not satisfied within a week that appropriate measures are being taken, we will consult our attorneys.

    Please assure us by return mail that you are taking steps to resolve these problems.

                    Sincerely,

                    John Smith

                    John Smith

Complaint to a supplier —
scheduling

A.B.C., Incorporated
One Main Street, U.S.A.
(555) 555-5555

Dear   :

    We value our business relationship with you. That is why we are concerned about your recent price increase.

    At our invitation, you submitted a bid for the housekeeping services at our offices. We accepted that bid on August 15. After three months of satisfactory performance, you have raised your monthly invoices by 5 percent. You informed us by telephone that this was not a mistake, asserting that rising costs necessitated the increase.

    Nothing in our contract, however, allows a unilateral price increase. We are enclosing a check for the contract price as payment in full. If you feel a price increase is justified, please negotiate this with us as specified in the contract.

              Sincerely,

              John Smith

              John Smith

Complaint to a contractor — prices

CANCELLING A CONTRACT

Every so often, due to circumstances beyond your or the supplier's control, a contract must be cancelled. Usually a brief, polite letter will do the trick. Occasionally the matter gets sticky, in which case a lawyer or legal department should be consulted.

Tips on How to Customize Your Letter:

1. State the cancellation in the first sentence.

2. Give a clear, concise reason for the cancellation.

3. Keep your tone on a professional level in the writing, and avoid attacking the supplier.

4. Express regret.

Optional Paragraphs and Phrases:

• Please cancel our order #2345.

• As we expressed in our letter of _____ , we are forced to make the contract null and void due to the extreme delay of the completion of the project.

• We no longer find a need for an in-house coffee machine. Please cancel our on-going order and remove the machine from the premises.

• We are sorry to have to come to this decision, but as a business owner yourself, we are sure you would make the same choice if you were in the same circumstance.

• Please be assured that this particular cancellation does not reflect our opinion of your work standards on a permanent basis.

• We do regret not being able to continue working with you on this project. Perhaps we will be able to work together in the future.

• Confirming our telephone conversation this morning, we are cancelling our order for _____ .

• Though we regret having to take this action, we have no choice but to cancel our contract.

• We are sure that an experienced businessman such as yourself will understand why we must cancel this order.

• Despite your repeated assurance, we still do not have the materials we ordered. We have obtained the materials elsewhere and hereby cancel our contract with you.

A.B.C., Incorporated
One Main Street, U.S.A.
(555) 555-5555

Dear   :

    Since you have taken no steps to bring your performance into
compliance with our contract, we have no alternative but to
cancel the contract.

    As you know, timely completion of the rehabilitation project
is an important part of our contract. We must seek a contractor
who can finish the work in a timely manner.

    We regret having to cancel this contract, but you should be
aware that we have no alternative.

               Sincerely,

               John Smith

               John Smith

Cancelling a contract

THANKING THE SUPPLIER

The tendency in this day and age, unfortunately, is to quickly air complaints and problems, but to keep surprisingly silent when a job is done well. Suppliers, just like employees and colleagues need to know when they have done well for you. Not only will a letter of thanks or a compliment make the suppliers feel good, it will make him or her want to do an even better job for you in the future.

Tips on How to Customize Your Letter:

1. Be sincere. Don't just compliment for the sake of a compliment.

2. List the specific people involved in the processing of the order, the sales effort, the construction work, if at all possible.

3. Be sure to specify the project or order involved. Undoubtedly these letters get filed away for future reference and the more specific the better.

4. Very often, your thoughtfulness in complimenting or thanking a helpful supplier will lead to more of the same kind of exceptional service, and perhaps some unexpected discounts and special attention. Be specific in your compliment, and sincere in its delivery.

5. If nothing else, this letter builds a bridge of goodwill. You'll surprise the person who receives the letter; so don't be surprised yourself when they return your call or letter with the comment, "Your letter floored me. In 20 years of business, nobody's ever taken time to do that".

Optional Paragraphs and Phrases:

• This has been quite a high pressure project. I want you to know that your company has come through so well for us, our admiration cannot adequately be expressed.

• We are especially impressed with the work of _____ , _____ , and _____ on the swift order processing and delivery of our materials.

• Thank you for your loyal cooperation and patience. The project could not have been completed with the level of success it has enjoyed without the efforts of all of your people.

• Please pass along our special thanks to _____ , _____ , _____ , and the entire construction crew.

• Needless to say, we look forward to a long and successful relationship with _____ (name company).

A.B.C., Incorporated
One Main Street, U.S.A.
(555) 555-5555

Dear   :

It is rare in this business to find a consistently outstanding vendor who routinely bends over backward to give more service than we contracted for, with more friendliness than we have a right to expect, plus the persistence and ingenuity to overcome the small, nagging little problems others would ignore.

Please give particular thanks to Bill Johnson, Sandy Hardy, and Carl O'Heirn for their tireless service on our account. We are looking forward to many more years of a mutually profitable relationship with these people and with your organization.

Sincerely,

John Smith

Thanking the vendor

LETTER COMPLIMENTING SUPPLIER

Just as you would be proud of your staff if they received a compliment from a client, the manager of one of your suppliers' staffs would greatly appreciate a complimentary letter for a job well done. As we have said many times before, if a job is done well it deserves recognition above and beyond the standard.

Tips on How to Customize Your Letter:

1. Make your compliment right away.

2. Explain the part the reader and his or her staff had in the success of the project or incident.

3. Close with a reiteration of your appreciation and compliments.

Optional Paragraphs and Phrases:

• I have attended many, many conferences in my career, and never have I seen one run as smoothly as the one your staff conducted on _____ .

• We have published a good many books in our time. We were still incredibly impressed by the quality of your typesetting work. Thank you for enabling us to publish a near perfect book.

• When we contracted to build a warehouse for _____ , we knew we could do it. What we didn't know is that we could do it for less than the budgeted amount and in half the time. The only factor that made this incredible feat possible was the great pride in the workmanship of your staff.

• Thank you again for making our stay so delightful. Please let us return the favor when you come to our neck of the woods.

• Please hear us when we say never have we been so impressed by such excellent quality of work.

• Our meeting was a smashing success, and we owe a great deal of that success to your staff. The preliminary work can make or break a meeting, and your planning was excellent.

• We have tried a number of locations for our activities, and none of them seemed to work. Then we had our latest meeting in your facility and everything seemed to work beautifully.

• It's difficult to find an organization that realizes the importance of repeat customers. But we've found one in you. Your planning and hospitality made our convention go smoothly, and I'm sure we will hold future events at your facility.

• Last week we had our annual convention at your hotel. Last night our executive committee decided to book next year's convention at your hotel as soon as possible. Please reserve your facility for our convention during the week of November 6.

A.B.C., Incorporated
One Main Street, U.S.A.
(555) 555-5555

Dear   :

I have received many compliments on this year's annual
convention of the State Association of Women Entrepreneurs. Most
of these compliments are the result of the courteous and efficient services provided by you and your hotel staff.

For many years I have been involved with the association and
have been to a number of the annual conventions. I do not think
any convention went as smoothly or received as many compliments
as this one.

Please accept my appreciation and extend it to your staff.

Sincerely,

Joan Smith

Joan Smith

Letter complimenting supplier

CHAPTER 13

Requesting Credit

In most situations, opening a line of credit with a supplier is a smarter financial move than paying cash up front. Keep in mind when corresponding with your current or prospective creditors how you expect your credit customers to correspond with you (see chapter 14).

Letters written to people you owe can be just as challenging as letters written to people who owe you. You want to sell the lender on the idea that you are an excellent credit risk and represent good business. Help your creditors feel secure and assure them that timely payment will be made. Be direct in answering questions when asked as ultimately you hurt yourself by avoiding or misrepresenting pertinent facts about yourself or your company.

Your business needs a steady supply of goods and services in order to stay in business. However, your suppliers also need your business and a potential order can often give you the leverage you need. Good credit is a function of clear communication, especially when finances and payments are concerned.

LETTERS REQUESTING CREDIT

Many business executives have made millions of dollars with no cash outlay. This is the power of having credit. Fortunately, it is common for suppliers to extend credit. However, if you need to establish credit at the time of an order or prior to it, use the following tips in your written request.

Tips on How to Customize Your Letter:

1. Place your order and state your terms in the same letter.

2. If you just want to open a line of credit without an accompanying order, state the reason you feel qualified.

3. Give a quick synopsis of your financial situation.

4. Provide credit references in body of letter or attach.

5. Close with a request that they expedite application or advise immediately if further information is necessary.

Optional Paragraphs and Phrases:

• We would like to order four cases of XLS Cleaner on 60-day credit terms, and at the same time open a credit line for future purchases.

• ABC, Inc. was started over 40 years ago and has grown significantly since.

• The need for industrial cleansers and equipment has always been a strong one, and in recent years it has become even stronger.

• For information concerning our financial standing and responsibilities, I refer you to the following:

• We are looking forward to establishing an ongoing and lucrative relationship for us both.

A.B.C., Incorporated
One Main Street, U.S.A.
(555) 555-5555

Dear   :

    We expect to submit purchase orders to you within the next few months. To make these purchases, however, we need trade credit.

    Our credit history is quite good and surely meets your credit standards. Enclosed are three credit references for your information. Please tell us as soon as possible if you need any more information before opening an account for us.

                     Sincerely,

                     John Smith

                     John Smith

Requesting credit — prior to order

A.B.C., Incorporated
One Main Street, U.S.A.
(555) 555-5555

Dear   :

    We have purchased goods from you for some time. The terms
have always been payment in full on delivery.

    Now we would like to open a credit account with you. Please
tell us what information you need to open an account for us.

                Sincerely,

                John Smith

                John Smith

Requesting credit — open account

A.B.C., Incorporated
One Main Street, U.S.A.
(555) 555-5555

Dear   :

    We are glad to submit the financial information and three references you requested.

    I hope you will expedite the credit investigation as we are reaching the point where we must have the order filled. If you have any questions or need additional information, please get in touch.

                Sincerely,

                John Smith

                John Smith

Letter sending credit information

LETTER NOTIFYING CREDITOR OF LATE PAYMENT

Occasionally cash flow is tight and a few bills are left temporarily unpaid. If such a situation should arise, it can help to write to your supplier and explain the situation. This will at least notify them that you are not intentionally avoiding payment. You would certainly appreciate the same courtesy from your credit customers.

Tips on How to Customize Your Letter:

1. State your case right up front. No beating around the bush.

2. Give a brief explanation of the situation. No need to go into the gory details, but give the reader a basic understanding of the problem.

3. Make an assurance at the end that the payment will be made as quickly as possible. If you can assign a date, do so.

Optional Paragraphs and Phrases:

• I am sorry to say that we've run into a problem and our payment is going to be late this month.

• As much as I hate to do this, I need an extension on my payment this month due to unforeseen and irreparable circumstances.

• We deeply appreciate your understanding and patience, and will do everything in our power to ensure that such a situation does not happen again.

• We will have the payment to you by _____ , and not one day later.

• Again, accept our apologies and thanks for your cooperation.

A.B.C., Incorporated
One Main Street, U.S.A.
(555) 555-5555

Dear   :

    I regret having to tell you that we are unable to make this month's payment on our account.

    As you know, one of our biggest customers just went into bankruptcy reorganization because of the unexpected death of its founder. We and the other creditors are working to bring the business through this trying period, and we think our efforts will be successful. Our success, however, hinges on the efforts of secondary creditors such as you.

    Rest assured that you will receive whatever payments we can make, and we will begin making full payments on account as soon as we can. Thank you for your cooperation.

        Sincerely,

        John Smith

        John Smith

Letter notifying creditor of late payment

LETTERS TO CREDITORS

Since very often letters to creditors cover embarrassing subjects such as overdue accounts or inability to pay, the best bet is to keep them short and sweet. Get to the point, express your regret/appreciation and close the letter.

Tips on How to Customize Your Letter:

1. Be apologetic, but not overwhelming.

2. Explain the situation clearly, but briefly.

3. Ask for understanding and cooperation.

4. Promise to make amends in as quick a time as possible.

5. Close with one more expression of regret.

Optional Paragraphs and Phrases:

- We are very sorry we will not be able to make our interest payment this month.

- We are terribly embarrassed about check #123456 which was returned to you by the bank.

- Our warehouse was severely damaged by the recent brush fires in our area. The extensive damage has set us back financially. We are asking all of our creditors to be patient with us for just a short while until we recover from this devastation.

- We contacted the bank immediately, because we were unaware of any depletion of funds in that account. The bank, as it turned out was in error, and will send you a replacement check this week.

- From our past record, I'm sure you realize we would not be writing this type of letter unless it was a dire emergency.

- Thank you so much for your understanding. Please be assured that within two weeks we should have recovered enough to pay what is owed to you.

- Enclosed is partial payment of invoice # _____ . Because a number of items we received were damaged they were refused and are being shipped back to you.

- Financing of a major project has been stalled, and this financing snag has caused cash flow problems throughout our operation.

- As you might have heard, our president recently suffered a stroke. While we believe this will not affect the firm's long-term prospects, it has caused some temporary turmoil.

- This situation causes us as much discomfort as it causes you. Therefore we are working to make sure it is as short-lived as possible.

A.B.C., Incorporated
One Main Street, U.S.A.
(555) 555-5555

Dear   :

    I was shocked to hear that the check we sent you last week was returned by the bank for "insufficient funds." The check was No. 55407 and was for $8,790.36.

    Let me assure you that our finances are first-rate, and we are quite credit worthy. I discussed the matter with our bank manager, and he admitted that the bank was in error. You should soon receive a letter from him confirming this.

    Please redeposit the check, and it will clear with no problem. If you experience any problems like this in the future, please let me know immediately.

            Sincerely,

            John Smith

            John Smith

Letter to a creditor — returned check

COMPLAINT TO A CREDIT BUREAU

Even though the most common correspondence to a credit bureau is in the form of an inquiry, every once in a while a credit bureau will do something that needs to be brought to their attention.

Tips on How to Customize Your Letter:

1. Be clear.

2. Specify your complaint and offer any necessary details.

3. Be polite and don't attack, even though the credit bureau is at fault.

Optional Paragraphs and Phrases:

• We received a report from one of our vendors that you sent them a letter stating that we are extremely delinquent on a certain account.

• Unfortunately, there must be an error in your records or information source. As you can see from the enclosed copies of all bills and checks attached to that account, we are completely up-to-date.

• Please correct this error as soon as possible and send a correction to the vendor in question.

• This situation has made obtaining further credit very difficult, if not impossible for us. We would appreciate greatly if it were rectified immediately.

• Thank you so much for your attention to this matter. We will be in contact to follow up on the outcome next week.

• Our disagreement with this creditor was settled some months ago. It is unfortunate that the creditor informed you of our initial refusal to pay but failed to let you know of the final adjustment in our favor.

• Our credit rating is a valuable and hard-won asset. We would appreciate your restoring it to us as soon as possible

A.B.C., Incorporated
One Main Street, U.S.A.
(555) 555-5555

Dear   :

    We recently were denied credit by one of our suppliers based on a report issued by your office. As we understand it, your report states that we are six months overdue on one of our accounts payable.

    We know of no account on which we are overdue at all. Nor can we recall being six months overdue on any account.

    Naturally we are concerned about this error and must have it resolved immediately. Please correct our credit report and send us a copy immediately.

                Sincerely,

                John Smith

Complaint to a credit bureau

CHAPTER 14

Granting Credit

Credit is the lifeblood of most businesses. It is difficult to do business today without giving credit to customers.

A letter asking for credit information can be difficult to write in order to convey both firmness and diplomacy. You might not be able to make the sale without granting credit, but there's no point in making a credit sale unless you will get a check that clears the bank.

Collection letters can be equally difficult to write. As a creditor you want to make it clear that you expect payment as soon as possible, but you don't want to be inflexible. Even a solid, well-run business can suffer temporary cash flow problems. You don't want to be inflexible or abusive to a customer at the risk of losing the customer's business.

Many of these problems are reduced if you establish a firm policy that is applied routinely and consistently to all customers and potential debtors. Letters should be simple and factual. The customer should be informed that his patronage is desired, but that he must maintain certain standards if he wants to receive credit.

All credit information is confidential. As a rule you should either not reveal credit information without a customer's permission or should consult an attorney for the details of federal and state privacy laws. Both federal and state laws regulate collection practices. Before establishing a collection policy, you should be fully briefed on the laws of privacy, harassment, and libel.

ASKING FOR CREDIT INFORMATION

Having the proper information before you grant any customer credit is vital to the financial health of your company. It can be a little awkward, however, asking for such information to be supplied by the customer. Simply make the collection of complete credit information part of your business practices and then tell the applying customer just that. People usually have no problems when a request is part of normal procedure; it is when they feel singled out that they may be insulted.

Tips on How to Customize Your Letters:

1. Thank the customer for his or her order.

2. Explain the reason behind the need for credit information. (They are a first time customer, or the order is such a large one.)

3. Enclose easy to use forms to ensure minimal inconvenience on the customer's part and a complete collection of proper information on yours. (If this is done from the beginning it eliminates the necessity for embarrassing follow-up.)

4. Be sure to project the feeling of a routine operation.

5. Close by assuring confidentiality and speed in processing.

Optional Paragraphs and Phrases:

- Thank you so much for your order for three of our latest Model 513s.

- We are pleased to see your request for credit payment on your order, and will process your request as soon as possible.

- In order to process your credit application as quickly as possible and ship your order immediately, we need just a few pieces of information as a routine formality.

- Enclosed please find our standard credit application. Please fill it out completely and return it to our business office address.

- Of course, all information you furnish us with will be kept in the strictest confidence and will be processed immediately.

A.B.C., Incorporated
One Main Street, U.S.A.
(555) 555-5555

Dear   :

    Thank you for your recent order. The shipment you requested
is being processed now.

    We noticed that this is your first order, so we are enclos-
ing an application for a credit line. If you will complete the
form and return it as soon as possible, there should be no delay
in shipping your order.

    This information is strictly confidential and for our
internal use only.

    We are glad to have you as a customer and look forward to a
long and mutually rewarding relationship.

               Sincerely,

               John Smith

               John Smith

A.B.C., Incorporated
One Main Street, U.S.A.
(555) 555-5555

Dear   :

    We received your recent order and are very pleased to have you as a customer. In order to carry out the transaction, we need your help.

    Unfortunately, some information we need is not available through our regular channels. I am sure you understand why we cannot process an order until our records are complete. Please complete the enclosed information form and return it to us in the enclosed postpaid envelope. All information will be held in strict confidence.

    It will take approximately three weeks to complete our records, yet your order requests immediate fulfillment. We can comply with this request if you include a check for $ when returning the information form.

              Sincerely,

              John Smith

              John Smith

REQUESTS FOR CREDIT REFERENCE

Tips on How to Customize Your Letters:

1. State your request and who the credit applicant is in the first paragraph.

2. Refrain from mentioning the specifics of the purchase or the credit arrangement. There is no need for anyone but you and the credit applicant to know about these things.

3. Make it easy for the reader to respond by enclosing a self-addressed, postage-paid envelope.

4. Assure the reader that all information provided will be kept in the strictest confidence.

5. Offer to reciprocate the gesture.

Optional Paragraphs and Phrases:

• I have received a request for credit privileges from _____ in _____, owner _____ .

• Your company has been listed as a credit reference.

• I would be very grateful if you could supply the following information about this customer:

• The following information is needed in order to complete this customer credit check: credit terms extended to this customer; customer's promptness in meeting obligations; your reservations, if any, about the customer's financial standing.

• Please be assured that any and all information you can give us will be kept in the strictest confidence.

• Please return the information to the above business office address at your earliest convenience.

• Please return this and any other information you consider pertinent in the enclosed postage-paid envelope.

• Any information we could use to evaluate this credit application is welcome. We are particularly interested in the duration of the relationship and the consistency of payments.

• We understand that ABC, Inc. has a credit account with you. ABC has applied for a $15,000 credit line with us, and we would appreciate your opinion of their ability to service this obligation.

• Our credit reporting form is enclosed along with a pre-stamped envelope. The form is designed so it can be completed in just a few minutes. We are grateful for both your time and assistance on this matter.

A.B.C., Incorporated
One Main Street, U.S.A.
(555) 555-5555

Dear   :

    Your name was given to us as a credit reference for the XYZ Company of 822 East Baltimore Street.

    We would appreciate your completing the enclosed form and returning it to us in the pre-addressed envelope. Any additional comments you care to make also would be appreciated. If you prefer, I would be glad to take this information over the telephone. All information will be considered strictly confidential.

    Thank you for your attention to this matter, and we will be glad to reciprocate whenever we can.

               Sincerely,

               John Smith

               John Smith

Request for credit reference —
form enclosed

A.B.C., Incorporated
One Main Street, U.S.A.
(555) 555-5555

Dear   :

    We received a credit application from the XYZ Company of 822
East Baltimore Street, and they listed you as a credit reference.

    We would appreciate your telling us how long XYZ Company has
had a credit account with you, whether or not the relationship is
satisfactory, and the average outstanding balance of the account.
Any other information you care to add is welcome.

    This information is, of course, confidential. Thank you for
your assistance.

                              Sincerely,

                              John Smith

                              John Smith

*Request for credit reference —
no form enclosed*

A.B.C., Incorporated
One Main Street, U.S.A.
(555) 555-5555

Dear   :

    Your bank was given to us as a reference by the above-referenced firm. We would appreciate any information you can give us on the firm and its financial standing.

    Since we are considering an extension of credit to this company, we are especially interested in its record of handling its accounts payable. Of course, any general comments you have about the firm and its management would be appreciated.

    Any information you give us will be treated as confidential and will be greatly appreciated.

                Sincerely,

                John Smith

                John Smith

Reference inquiry to a banker

INQUIRY TO A CREDIT BUREAU

Tips on How to Customize Your Letter:

1. Explain clearly what you are looking for.

2. If time is of the essence, make sure that the reader understands that.

3. Be polite and explain briefly why you need this particular information.

Optional Paragraphs and Phrases:

• We are considering a substantial contract with XYZ Electronics Corp., and would like as much information about their organization as possible before we sign the contract.

• Please send us a complete credit history on XYZ Electronics Corp. of Santa Barbara, CA as soon as possible.

• We are in a bit of a pinch and need your help. XYZ Electronics Corp. has offered us an excellent opportunity, but we need to give them an answer by next Friday for the deal to be ours. Before we go ahead with the contract, we would like some information on their organization. Could you please rush us what you have by Monday, p.m.?

• Thank you so much for the extra effort you made in getting our information to us so promptly. It is very much appreciated.

• We extend credit only to firms with top credit ratings. Please let us know anything that keeps this firm from having a top rating.

A.B.C., Incorporated
One Main Street, U.S.A.
(555) 555-5555

Dear   :

   We would like credit information on DEF Corporation of
Greenville, South Carolina. This firm has made a rather substantial rush order of our products.

   If this company is financially sound, their business could
be very important to our firm. Therefore, it is important that
we receive this information quickly so that we can make a decision before DEF seeks another supplier.

   Thank you for your attention.

                              Sincerely,

                              John Smith
                              John Smith

Inquiry to a credit bureau

LETTER GRANTING CREDIT

Acceptance letters are always pleasurable ones to write, and usually they come easily to the mind of the writer. In this case, accepting someone for credit, you are happy because you are taking on a new substantial customer who is a good credit risk. And, the customer is happy to hear that he or she has been accepted for credit.

Tips on How to Customize Your Letter:

1. Tell the reader right away that they have been accepted.

2. Also mention that you did contact their references and that they found his or her credit history more than acceptable.

3. Enclose a standard credit agreement for them to sign.

4. Tell the customer how much you value his or her patronage and how happy you are that you could come to a good credit arrangement.

Optional Paragraphs and Phrases:

• According to our policy, we have checked with the references you supplied to us.

• The references you listed were all contacted. They have given a unanimous approval of your credit rating.

• We are more than happy to accept you as a credit customer of ours.

• Congratulations! You have officially opened a credit account (#1234567) with ABC Industries.

• We are pleased to extend you our most favorable credit terms. Customers like you are few and far between and we want to be sure that you are 100% satisfied.

• Please sign both copies of the enclosed credit agreement. Return one to us in the postage-paid envelope supplied for your convenience, and keep the other for your own records.

• We want you to know that we will always be ready to help you in any way, and are always at your service.

- We are so happy to include you in our growing family of satisfied customers. Please let us know if we can be of assistance in any other way.

- Your credit references were contacted and spoke highly of your firm. We are glad to open your account on our most favorable credit terms.

- We have heard from your credit references and are pleased to grant you credit. The limit on this account, however, is lower than what you asked for. Your firm has a good reputation in the financial community, and we believe that the credit limit can be raised in due time.

- The credit references you gave us spoke highly of your firm. Accordingly, we are glad to open your account with us and have shipped your initial order as you requested.

- We are pleased to grant you the credit line you asked for and look forward to a long relationship with you.

- We are glad to grant credit to you. But considering the amount of your other obligations and the credit you desire from us, we will need collateral for any credit we extend.

A.B.C., Incorporated
One Main Street, U.S.A.
(555) 555-5555

Dear   :

It is a pleasure to open your account with a maximum credit line of $. We contacted your credit references and found your credit history to be very satisfactory.

Enclosed are two copies of our standard credit agreement. Please sign one and return it to us. The other is for your records.

We very much value you as a customer and will be as cooperative and flexible as we can. If you have any problems with our services or products, do not hesitate to let us know immediately.

Sincerely,

John Smith

John Smith

Letter granting credit

LETTER DENYING CREDIT

Turning down an applicant for anything is not an easy thing to do. Turning a customer down for credit is exceptionally difficult because there is a chance of losing the customer. A well-thought-out rejection of credit letter can keep the applicant's business and goodwill as well. A poorly written one, on the other hand, may very well insult the reader and force him or her to take their business elsewhere.

Tips on How to Customize Your Letter:

1. Thank the reader immediately for their interest and order, if one has already gone through.

2. Be gentle when breaking the news on being turned down to the reader.

3. Never, ever use the terms "poor credit risk!"

4. Always leave hope in the reader's mind for future reevaluation and acceptance.

5. Leave option of doing business on a cash basis very clear in reader's mind.

Optional Paragraphs and Phrases:

- Thank you for your patience while we underwent our standard credit investigation.

- Thank you so much for your interest in ABC Industries.

- We truly appreciate your request to open a credit line with our organization. As you are probably aware by now, we have been undergoing our standard credit investigation for the past three weeks.

- We regret due to conflicting information from the references you supplied us, we must turn down your request for credit with our company.

- We will be very happy to reinvestigate, and reopen your application at some future time if you so desire.

- Until, then, we look forward to continuing our business association as it has been for the past few years.

- Although we cannot, at this time, extend credit to you, we want very much for you to join our family of customers.

- Please allow us to serve you in any way possible.

- Regrettably, we cannot approve your credit application. We received conflicting information in our inquiries and were unable to resolve these conflicts. This matter was pursued as far as we would take it, and a decision had to be made.

- The information we have forces us to conclude that your credit request should not be granted. We are not in a position to extend the amount of credit you desire.

- Our position is not fixed. We are glad to work with you and discuss this matter further as long as further discussions are profitable.

- If you want to discuss this matter further, we are always glad to consider any additional information you can provide.

- We sincerely want you as a customer and will do all we can to serve you and work out a mutually satisfactory long-term relationship.

- Your credit record is very impressive, and we would like to grant the terms you request. Such terms, however, are more favorable than any we have granted to our current customers. We do not believe it would be fair to our long-time customers to give any single firm special terms.

A.B.C., Incorporated
One Main Street, U.S.A.
(555) 555-5555

Dear   :

   Thank you for your order and credit application.

   Based on the information we received, we cannot approve your
credit line. We are very pleased with your interest in our
products and would like to have you as a customer. Therefore, if
you believe our action is not justified or can supply additional
information, we want to hear from you. In the meantime, please
feel free to continue using our services on a cash basis as you
have to date.

   We will be as flexible and cooperative as possible and look
forward to establishing a long-term relationship with you.

                              Sincerely,

                              John Smith

                              John Smith

Letter denying credit

LETTER NOTIFYING DEBTOR OF RETURNED CHECK

A returned check is a source of strife and annoyance for both you and the customer who paid with the bad check. The best way to handle such a situation is quickly, directly, and as painlessly as possible.

Tips on How to Customize Your Letter:

1. Open the letter with the problem and the specific invoice, check # and amount of money involved.

2. Offer the reader an out by saying that you are sure there's some simple explanation or inadvertent error at the root of the problem. Do not assume deliberate fraud.

3. State clearly and politely that you must receive payment of _____ now.

4. Close the letter by thanking the reader for his understanding and/or cooperation.

5. Enclose copy of returned check with letter to verify problems to customer and assure him he is not paying twice. Retain bad check in your files for legal documentation later should it be necessary to sue for payment.

A.B.C., Incorporated
One Main Street, U.S.A.
(555) 555-5555

Dear   :

    Your Check No.   in the amount of $ has been
returned to us by the bank marked...[insufficient funds, account
closed, etc].

    Therefore, it is vital that we receive a certified check or
money order as a replacement from you by return mail.

    I am sure that if this incident is the result of a simple
error, you will send us the replacement as soon as possible. If
you are experiencing temporary financial difficulties, please let
me know. We want to do whatever we can to help out. It is
important that you act quickly to maintain your good credit
record.

    Thank you for your cooperation.

                Sincerely,

                John Smith
                John Smith

*Letter notifying debtor of
returned check*

COLLECTION PROCESS—SERIES OF THREE LETTERS

The steps of a collection process actually coordinate nicely with human emotion. Initially you remind the reader to pay (benefit of the doubt), then you inquire as to any problem there might be (curiosity), and finally you demand payment (frustration). The number of letters you use depends on the time you have to extend your cash, your patience, and the time you have to write letters.

Tips on How to Customize Your Letters:

1. Try not to write any letter in anger, at least don't let the letter have an angry tone.

2. Be specific. State amount due, age of bill (30, 60, 90 days old, etc.) and refer to specific open invoices in question.

3. Use "you" and "your" as often as possible. (It's a subtle way to point the finger!)

Optional Paragraphs and Phrases:

• Just wanted to quickly remind you that your account is now past due for _____ .

• Bills are always hard to remember to pay. We thought we'd do you a favor and remind you of ours which was due _____ for the amount of _____ .

• If you've already taken care of the payment for invoice #2345 which was due _____ for the amount of _____ , please disregard this notice.

• We need your help so we can continue to provide the quality service and product you've been accustomed to. Please pay your bill which was due _____ for the amount of _____ .

• Is something wrong? Are you having a problem with your order or our service? We can't think of why else you did not respond to our other reminder notices for your bill which was due _____ .

• Is there a problem we should know about? If there is a problem affecting your payment, please notify us right away so we can make some arrangements.

• We are having a difficult time understanding why you have not paid your bill, and have not responded to any of our reminders. This has not happened before and we are concerned. Please let us know what the situation is.

• You have now received _____ notices from us regarding your bill of _____ . Unless we receive remittance by _____ we will be forced to stop your credit.

• We appreciate being reminded that one of our payments is past due. So we're sending this brief reminder that your account balance of _____ is now past due.

• Your account balance of _____ is now past due. Please take care of this today so we won't be bothering you with any more letters.

• While reviewing your account, we noticed that it is now overdue.

- We still have not received payment despite our prior requests for settlement of your overdue account. To avoid unpleasantness, you must give this matter prompt attention and submit payment at once.

- We've found that one or two reminders is sufficient to bring an account up to date. You, however, have ignored all of our correspondence.

- If your payment of _____ for invoice # _____ is not received by us in 10 days, we will find it necessary to turn your account over to our collection agency.

- We do not understand your failure to respond to our prior letters. Your account is now long past due. We must request that you submit payment by return mail.

- We've always had your cooperation in the past and are puzzled that you have not seen fit to respond to our previous reminders. We expect either payment from you within 10 days or some explanation for the delay.

- This is our final request for payment. If we do not receive payment within seven business days your delinquency will be reported to the local credit bureau. As you know, this will damage your credit standing and hinder your ability to get additional credit.

- This is our final request for payment. If we do not receive payment within seven days, your account will be turned over to our attorneys for collection.

A.B.C., Incorporated
One Main Street, U.S.A.
(555) 555-5555

Dear   :

     We are sure it is probably an oversight but would like to
remind you that you have an open account with us in the amount of
$ which is now 60 days old.

     Since this exceeds our agreed on credit terms, we would
appreciate your prompt cooperation and payment.

     If there is any question regarding the bill or you have a
problem, please contact us immediately.

     Your attention to this matter would be greatly appreciated.

               Sincerely,

               John Smith

               John Smith

Initial collection letter

A.B.C., Incorporated
One Main Street, U.S.A.
(555) 555-5555

Dear   :

    Despite past notices to you, a balance of $ remains
long overdue (90 days).

    We have enjoyed a very pleasant business relationship with
you and certainly want nothing to change it; but we are becoming
quite concerned.

    If circumstances prevent immediate payment, please contact
us by phone or mail to work out the problem. We may be able to
suggest something that will be helpful.

    Unless we hear from you, we must unfortunately assume there
is nothing further we can do to resolve the problem. If the
account is taken from our control, your good credit history will
be jeopardized.

    We look forward to hearing from you this week.

                        Sincerely,

                        John Smith

                        John Smith

A.B.C., Incorporated
One Main Street, U.S.A.
(555) 555-5555

Dear   :

    We have received no response to our previous reminders that
your account is past due.

    This is your final notice. Unless we have full payment for
$ within the next ten days, your account will be turned
over for collection.

    Your attention to this matter is essential and in your best
interest. Please act now.

                          Sincerely,

                          John Smith
                          John Smith

A.B.C., Incorporated
One Main Street, U.S.A.
(555) 555-5555

Dear   :

    We believe that we have been very cooperative in accepting
the repayment you proposed a few months ago and expected that you
would be able to reduce your past due balance gradually while
keeping the rest of the account current.

    Unfortunately, you have been unable to do this, and we must
hereby suspend further credit. Therefore, new orders will
require cash with order until the entire balance in your present
account is made current. We expect regular repayments under the
terms previously agreed upon. If terms are met and debt cleared,
we will be glad to reinstate your credit line.

                Sincerely,

                John Smith
                John Smith

Letter suspending further credit

LETTERS ACKNOWLEDGING PAYMENT FOR OVERDUE ACCOUNT

Sometimes it is appropriate to acknowledge when an overdue account gets paid. The communication to the customer will ease their mind, and hopefully avoid any further delinquency from the same customer. It is important to note that these letters are not necessary in all cases, only when you feel the need to clear the slate or when the customer has requested acknowledgement.

Tips on How to Customize Your Letter:

1. Express your pleasure and the fact that the payment was received in the first paragraph.

2. Explain any restrictions that have been lifted.

3. Reinforce the terms of the credit agreement you have with the customer, especially the term about when payment is due.

4. End on another thank you and reassurance of a continuing relationship.

Optional Paragraphs and Phrases:

- Thank you for your payment. We received it on _____ .

- Your credit with us is once again available for your use.

- Please reread the credit agreement you signed with us. Pay careful attention to the clause about when each payment is due. I think we both want to make certain that your credit does not have to be disrupted again.

- Again, we greatly appreciate your payment and sincerely hope that a similar situation does not occur again.

- We look forward to a long and satisfying supplier/customer relationship with you.

A.B.C., Incorporated
One Main Street, U.S.A.
(555) 555-5555

Dear   :

    I am pleased to acknowledge receipt of your recent payment and announce that your credit line is reinstated.

    We have reinstated the credit line with its previous terms and with the understanding that payment is due when the statement is received. The terms are stated in detail in the initial credit agreement you signed and should have on file.

    We appreciate your payment and look forward to a continuation of our mutually rewarding relationship.

              Sincerely,

              John Smith

              John Smith

Letter reinstating credit

A.B.C., Incorporated
One Main Street, U.S.A.
(555) 555-5555

Dear   :

    I am glad to acknowledge receipt of your recent payment for
$. This leaves a past due balance of $.

    We appreciate this payment and are sure only something
critical would keep you from making full payment and will
cooperate as much as we can during this period of financial
stress. We do require, however, either a partial payment or a
note explaining its absence every 30 days.

    Please help us work with you toward a resolution of this
problem.

              Sincerely,

              John Smith

Letter acknowledging partial payment

A.B.C., Incorporated
One Main Street, U.S.A.
(555) 555-5555

Dear   :

    I was glad to hear from you regarding your account with us.

    We are satisfied with the plan you propose for repaying the balance of $. You will receive regular monthly statements that conform to the plan you proposed. We are confident you proposed this plan in good faith and will gradually reduce your past due amount while keeping the current balance up to date.

    Please understand that we fully expect this new commitment schedule to be met regardless of any conditions or circumstances.

    If there is anything else we can do to help, please let us know.

                 Sincerely,

                 John Smith

                 John Smith

Letter accepting payment adjustments

LETTER APOLOGIZING FOR ERRONEOUS COLLECTION LETTER

We all make mistakes, there's no way to get around that. But, when we do, the best remedy is admission. It is especially important to admit to a customer that you have accidently sent them a collection letter. If you are straightforward and honest in your apology, more often than not the customer will accept the mistake graciously, and even think all the better of you for your personal and sincere treatment of an error.

Tips on How to Customize Your Letters:

1. Apologize, but don't go overboard. It is an error, not a felony.

2. Be very brief and very sincere.

3. Apologize for the inconvenience, because incorrect collection letters do tend to cause quite a stir.

4. Promise the customer to the best of your ability that such an error will be avoided in the future.

Optional Paragraphs and Phrases:

- We apologize for the collection letter we sent you last week. It was sent to you in error.

- Oh my! When we make a mistake it is rare, but it is a big one!

- Please accept our deepest apologies for the collection letter sent to you in error last month.

- As our track record shows, we do try our utmost to avoid errors. Unfortunately we let this one slip by. We are sorry for any inconvenience the incorrect collection letter may have caused you.

- Please accept my word when I say that every possible precaution is and will continue to be taken to avoid such an error from happening again.

- You are one of our most valued customers. I am doubly embarrassed that we could have inconvenienced you of all people.

- Please accept the enclosed book of special discount coupons as a token of our deepest apologies.

- We certainly hope you forgive our error.

- Thank you for your patience and understanding.

A.B.C., Incorporated
One Main Street, U.S.A.
(555) 555-5555

Dear   :

I hope you will accept my sincere apology for the erroneous
letter we sent you.

We do not make mistakes very often, but when we do they are
big ones! You have a top-notch payment record, and the letter we
sent you was totally inappropriate.

We will take every precaution to ensure that this sort of
error does not happen again.

Sincerely,

John Smith

Apology — general

A.B.C., Incorporated
One Main Street, U.S.A.
(555) 555-5555

Dear   :

    As you know, the collection notice we sent you last week was sent in error. Your account is in better order than our accounting records.

    Please accept our sincere apology for this error. We do our best to eliminate errors, but they occasionally creep in. I hope this mistake has not caused you any inconvenience or embarrassment.

        Sincerely,

        John Smith

Apology — collection

CHAPTER 15

Dealing with Finances

All of the letters in this book are geared to help your business improve its financial position by creating sales, cash flow, goodwill, etc.

The letters in this chapter specifically deal with your business's finances and financing. These letters are addressed to banks, insurance companies, money managers, and other companies that will either handle your money or help finance your business.

Letters of this nature should be concise and direct. When financial matters are involved, you will want to avoid the use of attention-getting writing or other gimmicks. Be conservative and professional. Talk as one businessperson to another.

LETTERS COMMUNICATING WITH BANKS

Letters to banks are usually requests for information or detailed instructions. They should be written clearly, but graciously. It's always a good idea to maintain a good relationship with the bank!

Tips on How to Customize Your Letters:

1. Use language that is simple and easy to understand. Formal language is definitely outdated.

2. Be specific with the point you want to make.

3. Be extra careful to express clearly exactly what it is you are looking for.

Optional Paragraphs and Phrases:

• We have been banking with you for many years now and have always received our monthly statements at the beginning of the month. The past three statements have arrived two weeks into the month. We are wondering if there has been a change in your policies.

• Please send us any information you have on opening employee profit-sharing accounts with your bank.

• We are interested in adding company-paid IRAs to our benefit plan. Please send us information on the IRAs available through your bank and what the current rates are.

• Please let us know at your earliest convenience if there is anything else you need to know before answering our request.

• We are interested in establishing a banking relationship with an institution that can provide a lock box service and a seasonal line of credit.

• Please send us a description of your trust services and your fee schedule for pension funds. We are particularly interested in any special services for small corporations.

• It's become clear that you are not as optimistic about the firm's ability to grow as we are.

• While we can appreciate the need for your conservatism, we believe our firm should use a bank with a temperament closer to our own.

• We intend to continue a relationship with your bank. It offers several services that we believe are not available elsewhere.

A.B.C., Incorporated
One Main Street, U.S.A.
(555) 555-5555

Dear   :

    We are interested in developing a new banking relationship
and have received favorable comments about you from several other
businesses. Please let us know what arrangements you can offer.

    We are a small service business with about 15 employees that
generates a great deal of cash during the year. Last calendar
year we had gross revenues of approximately $3 million.

    Our sales, however, are seasonal. During our slow periods
we must have cooperation and patience from our bankers and
creditors. During our brisk periods a great deal of our sales
are made through the mail. Therefore, we would benefit greatly
from lock boxes or similar services.

    If you are interested in working with us, please contact me
so that we can discuss your services in detail.

                  Sincerely,

                  John Smith

*Letter establishing new
banking relationship*

A.B.C., Incorporated
One Main Street, U.S.A.
(555) 555-5555

Dear   :

    As you know, your bank has been our exclusive banker since we opened for business four years ago. This relationship has been a mutually enjoyable and profitable one, and we look forward to its continuing.

    Because of our firm's vigorous growth, however, we feel that some diversity is needed. Recent events have made it clear both to us and to you that there are times when you will be unable to satisfy our immediate needs. Therefore, on the advice of both outside consultants and the Board of Directors, we are moving two of our smaller accounts to another institution. You will soon receive details concerning the transfer of funds.

    I want to make it clear that we look forward to a long relationship with you. But it is clear to both of us that a firm of our size cannot limit itself to one financial institution. This additional flexibility should result in more revenues for our firm, which should be rewarding to both us and you.

    Please contact me if you wish to discuss this further.

                Sincerely,

                John Smith

Letter improving current banking services

A.B.C., Incorporated
One Main Street, U.S.A.
(555) 555-5555

Stop Payment Notice

Dear   :

    You are hereby directed to place a stop payment order and
refuse payment upon presentment of the following check:

    Name of Payee:

    Date of Check:

    Amount:

    Check Number:

    This stop order shall remain in effect until further written
notice.

                                  _____
                                  Name of Account

                                  _____
                                  Account Number

                                  By: _____

Stop payment notice

INQUIRY TO A FINANCIAL INSTITUTION

Letters to financial institutions can be requests for information, requests for services, appreciation for a service well done, or simply confirmation of agreements. The example shown here is of an inquiry, which is the most common type of correspondence to financial institutions.

Tips on How to Customize Your Letter:

1. If offering a compliment, be sincere; if registering a complaint or concern, be polite.

2. Always be concise and specific about the information and/or service you are asking about.

3. Offer a clear explanation of your position or situation to ensure the best understanding between yourself and the reader.

Optional Paragraphs and Phrases:

● We have heard that your organization recently completed an extensive study on mail order businesses in the United States. Being one of those companies, we would greatly appreciate information on how to obtain a copy of that study.

● You have been recommended to us as one of the leading consultants for setting employee benefit programs. We are in the midst of setting up such a program and would like more information on your services.

● We are upgrading our fringe benefit program and are inviting you to submit a proposal.

● As part of our employee benefits program we periodically invite experts in various aspects of personal finance to speak at a breakfast meeting of our executives. We would like to schedule a representative of your firm for a future meeting.

● We are very interested in providing comprehensive health services to our employees but believe this is possible for less than we are paying now.

A.B.C., Incorporated
One Main Street, U.S.A.
(555) 555-5555

Dear   :

    We are restructuring our employee benefits programs. As part of that restructuring we are considering the use of outside money managers for our various employee benefit trusts. We have heard favorable mention of your investment services and would like to hear what you can offer us.

    After the benefits programs are restructured, we will have a pension plan, profit-sharing plan, and an elective 401(k) plan. The cumulative net asset value of these funds will be approximately $3 million. Currently, I have served double duty as president of the corporation and manager of the employee benefits funds, but the funds now have reached the level where full-time professional management is needed.

    If you are interested in working with us, please send me a description of your service and fees, your performance record (covering at least the last five years), a summary of your investment philosophy, and a list of references.

    I look forward to hearing from you soon.

                Sincerely,

                John Smith

                John Smith

Inquiry to a financial institution

LETTER TO A PROSPECTIVE INVESTOR

The letter you write to a prospective investor is an important sales letter. In it you must sell to this prospect why he or she should invest in your company. And convincing someone to put down a large sum of money is no easy sell. Put all the credibility and professionalism into the letter you can, while making a strong pitch on the benefits to the investor.

Tips on How to Customize Your Letter:

1. Explain at the beginning of the letter how you heard of this person or company, any connections you might have, and why you are appealing to this particular party.

2. Then, go immediately into who you and your business are.

3. After that, explain why you're looking for investors.

4. Then, tell the reader what investing in your company will do for him or her.

5. Enclose as much material on your company as possible.

6. Close with the assumption that you will be meeting with the reader.

Optional Paragraphs and Phrases:

• Mr. _____ of _____ told me that you were looking to invest in some companies other than your own.

• Let me explain a little about ABC, Inc., our history, where we've been and where we're going...

• We are at a turning point in our growth pattern right now. We can no longer satisfy the demand for our products and services in our present facilities, but we need some more capital to expand adequately to plan for future growth.

• Our problem is, I believe, your venture.

• It's a happy problem to be faced with, no doubt. And, it will provide you with an opportunity for great financial growth.

• Thank you for your attention, and I look forward to meeting with you to discuss this matter in more detail.

• Our temporary cash flow problems were caused by the failure of a large customer and by some internal control problems. We have implemented solutions to both problems.

• We are looking for a silent partner to finance our expansion. Though we seek advice from a number of sources, we believe that the firm cannot be run competitively by a committee.

• Though this investment should be made for long-term capital growth, our accountant believes the investment can be structured to provide tax benefits for several years.

• Even under our best-case projections, cash cannot be taken out of the business for at least two years. This factor already has forced us to turn down two otherwise ideal investors.

A.B.C., Incorporated
One Main Street, U.S.A.
(555) 555-5555

Dear   :

   I was given your name by   , a mutual business
associate who might have mentioned our firm to you.

   A situation has arisen that creates an opportunity for you.
Our firm must finance an expansion with additional equity. We
are inviting outside investors to join our closely held corporation and share in this growth project.

   We are a rapidly growing manufacturer of specialty goods.
We produce goods that are designed by various retail firms and
are sold exclusively by them. A number of these products have
sold quite well, and we have generated a very good reputation
with some major national retailers. You probably have purchased
some of our products, and I have enclosed a list of them for your
reference.

   Demand for our services has escalated so rapidly, we are at
the point where we must expand our facilities or turn down work.
Since we have carved out a unique market niche, we want to avoid
turning down work if at all possible. The most profitable way of
handling this unique expansion opportunity is to allow investors
outside the company to take part in it.

   Enclosed are our most recent audited statements and a
description of our firm's history and operations. We are rather
flexible regarding the terms of the investment, but there are
some points we must insist on. These and other details can be
discussed at your convenience.

   I think the enclosed materials will convince you that this
is an extremely profitable use of your money. Please contact me
after you have reviewed the enclosed material, and we can pursue
this matter further.

                              Sincerely,   .

                              John Smith
                              John Smith

Letter to a prospective investor

RESPONDING TO A REJECTION OF LOAN APPLICATION

The objective of this letter is to leave the doors open. You may have been turned down this time, but perhaps sometime in the future you will need a loan again. The tone of this letter should be appreciative, considerate, and hopeful for the future.

Tips on How to Customize Your Letter:

1. Thank the reader for taking the time to consider your loan application.
2. Express your disappointment.
3. Emphasize how you hope to do business with them in the future.

Optional Paragraphs and Phrases:

- We appreciate your time in considering our loan application.

- The thoroughness of your investigation and analysis is impressive, and convinces me that your decision was a well educated one.

- Although we are disappointed that you felt unable to qualify us for the loan at this time, we bow to your judgment.

- We do have a few other applications under consideration and hope that one of them will be approved.

- Again, thank you for your time. We certainly hope that the future will bring an opportunity for us to do business together.

- Our view is that this firm now deserves a greater line of credit than you are willing to give it. We have received credit from you numerous times over the last five years and have always repaid the loans on schedule. We've shown that we can accurately judge our ability to repay.

- We are planning a major redeployment of assets and would appreciate a consultation with you so that the redeployment will enhance our ability to qualify for a loan in the future.

- We know that your job puts you in touch with many private investors. If you think any of these investors might be interested in financing this project, we'd appreciate your letting us know.

- Your understanding of our business is very apparent, so your opinion of this project has caused us to begin a reevaluation of it.

A.B.C., Incorporated
One Main Street, U.S.A.
(555) 555-5555

Dear   :

    I want to thank you for the time and effort you put into evaluating our application for a loan. It was obvious from the time I spent with you that a great deal of study and analysis went into your decision.

    It is unfortunate that we could not satisfy your standards for a loan. Your comments were fair, however, and we are modifying our policies and practices so that we will be able to qualify for a loan in the future. Several other financing sources are still considering our qualifications, and we think it is likely that something will come through soon.

    We appreciate your time and hope that we will be able to do business together in the future.

Sincerely,

John Smith

John Smith

Responding to rejection of
loan application

LETTER TO INSURANCE AGENCY

A letter to an insurance agency requesting information is similar to the one you might write to a financial institution. A polite, brief statement of your needs is all that is necessary.

Tips on How to Customize Your Letter:

1. Start off right away with why you are writing to this company.

2. Explain your current situation briefly.

3. Tell a little bit about your company to give the reader a point of reference.

4. Offer a meeting or time to review a proposal. Let the reader know you are serious.

Optional Paragraphs and Phrases:

• We seek a comprehensive property and casualty policy for our business. This policy should cover lost profits in addition to replacement of property.

• Our current policy is coming up for renewal. Please evaluate this policy and issue any proposal you wish us to consider.

• Please be sure that any policy you propose is underwritten by a company rated *A* or better by *Best's*.

• An important consideration to us is the amount of continuing service your agency will provide. Please let us know how you handle claims adjustment, policy reappraisal, and any other services you offer.

A.B.C., Incorporated
One Main Street, U.S.A.
(555) 555-5555

Dear   :

Our current group term and health insurance policies do not
quite meet our needs. Therefore, we are considering alternative
policies and would like you to submit one or more programs for
our consideration.

We are a small service business with 20 employees, but we
should grow to about 30 employees within 2 years at the most.
Seven of our employees qualify as owners, officers, or highly
compensated employees under IRS regulations. The employees are
rather young, with only one above age 45. We need a comprehensive policy that covers major medical, hospitalization,
maternity benefits, and dental care.

If you need additional information or have a proposal for us
to consider, contact me at your convenience. We would like to
choose a new insurance program by April 30.

Sincerely,

John Smith

John Smith

Letter to insurance agency

APPENDIX

A

Checklist for Effective Letters

All effective business letters have several features in common. For those who need to write a letter in a hurry, this checklist will ensure that you have all the essential ingredients.

☐ *Letterhead*

A business letter is written on well-designed letterhead. The letterhead should reveal basic information (firm's name, address, telephone number, and line of business) without attracting attention away from the body of the letter. The letterhead should reflect the type of image the firm is trying to convey. A business that wants to appear traditional and conservative (such as a law firm) would have a different design than a firm that thrives on creativity and originality (such as an interior design firm).

☐ *Paper*

Most business letters are written on 20 pound paper. A more elegant image is communicated with heavier paper. Lighter paper can be used on short notes.

☐ *Format*

There are several accepted letter formats, and the choice is up to the writer. Be sure that the format is attractive and easy to read. Details of formats are in the Introduction.

☐ *Inside Address*

Be sure that the inside address contains the correct name and job title of the addressee and his firm. Titles that precede a name (Mr., Mrs.) generally are not used in the inside address.

☐ *Salutation*

Your relationship to the reader dictates the proper salutation. Addressing the reader by his first name is correct when you know each other fairly well. Otherwise, when writing to an individual, use a proper form of address. When writing to a man, use "Dear Mr. _____ " or "Sir." When writing to a woman, use "Dear Ms. _____ " or "Madam."

If you don't know who will receive a letter, such as when you are writing to a firm or a department, an indefinite salutation is best. Unless you know the gender of the recipient, use "Dear Sir or Madam."

☐ *Lead Sentence*

This could be the most important part of the letter. It determines whether the letter is read closely or is skimmed. The opening sentence can make the reader interested in what you are saying, or it can turn off the reader before he's heard your message. Put a good deal of time into writing a lead that will capture the reader's interest.

☐ *Style*

The letter should be written in standard English, but it should not be written in formal English. Write as you talk, but be sure that you have complete sentences and that the grammar is correct.

☐ *Typographic Devices*

A letter can be made easier to read and certain points can be emphasized by the use of typographic devices. These devices include underlining, capitalization, bold type, different typefaces, different color ink, and indentation. The extent to which you use such devices depends largely on your own style and personality.

☐ *Paragraphs*

Be sure to divide the body of the letter into short, complete paragraphs. When you start a new thought, start a new paragraph. A one-sentence paragraph is better than a paragraph that takes up half the page.

☐ *Final Paragraph*

You want the reader to take some kind of action, and the last paragraph is where you get him to do it. Figure out ahead of time exactly what reaction you want from the addressee. Then put it in the last paragraph. As an alternative, the last paragraph can ask the reader to take an intermediate step that could lead to his taking the desired action.

☐ *Complimentary Close*

Most writers always use the same complimentary close and don't give much thought to it. They use the standard "Sincerely." Others search for a close that is uniquely theirs or captures a particular thought or emotion. Still other writers vary their closings. One closing will be used for those with whom they deal frequently and another is used in other correspondence.

☐ *Signature*

You decide whether to sign your full name or to establish a less formal relationship with the addressee by signing only your first name. Your full name is typed below the signature and your title or degrees you've earned can be typed either behind or below the name. Titles such as "Mr." or "Dr." are not used in either the signature or the typed name.

APPENDIX

B

How To Address VIPs

Occasionally you will write to public officials or other dignitaries. In such cases, it is important to use the correct title in the inside address and the salutation. Businessmen generally aren't sticklers about their titles, but many public officials are more closely attached to their titles and expect to be addressed properly. Usually when you write to a public official you are asking for something, so you should show the proper respect for his office.

This Appendix lists the proper titles and salutations for a number of public officials and other dignitaries.

Note about gender use. For convenience the designations below generally assume that the officeholder is male. In cases where the officeholder is a female, the use of "Mr." in the address or title is replaced by "Madam."

Federal Government Officials

Office	*Inside Address*	*Salutation*
President	The President	Dear Mr. President
Vice President	The Vice President of the United States	Dear Mr. Vice President
Chief Justice of the Supreme Court	The Chief Justice of the United States	Dear Mr. Chief Justice
Associate Justice of the Supreme Court	Mr. Justice Doe The Supreme Court of the United States	Dear Mr. Justice
Speaker of the House	The Honorable John Doe Speaker of the House of Representatives	Dear Mr. Speaker

Cabinet Official	The Honorable the Secretary of _____	Dear Mr. Secretary
	The Honorable the Ambassador to the UN	Dear Mr. Ambassador
	The Honorable the Director of the Office of Management and Budget	Dear Mr. Director
	The Honorable John Doe The Attorney General	Dear Mr. Attorney General
Postmaster General	The Honorable John Doe The Postmaster General	Dear Mr. Postmaster General
Cabinet Under Secretary	The Honorable John Doe Under Secretary of _____	Dear Mr. Doe
Senator	The Honorable John Doe United States Senate	Dear Senator Doe
Senate Committee Chairman	The Honorable John Doe, Chairman Committee on _____ United States Senate	Dear Mr. Chairman
Congressman	The Honorable John Doe House of Representatives	Dear Mr. Doe Dear Mr. Congressman
Head of Independent Commission or Agency	The Honorable John Doe Chairman, _____	Dear Mr. Chairman
Federal Judge	The Honorable John Doe Judge of the United States District Court for the _____ District of _____	Dear Judge Doe
Librarian of Congress	The Honorable John Doe Librarian of Congress	Dear Mr. Doe
Other High-Ranking Executive Officers	The Honorable John Doe Title	Dear Mr. Doe
Former Federal Government Officials	The Honorable John Doe	Dear Mr. Doe

State and Local Government Officials

Governor	The Honorable John Doe Governor of _____	Dear Governor Doe
Lieutenant Governor	The Honorable John Doe Lieutenant Governor of _____	Dear Mr. Doe
Secretary of State	The Honorable the Secretary of State	Dear Mr. Secretary

Attorney General	The Honorable John Doe	Dear Mr. Attorney General
Other State Officials and Representatives	The Honorable John Doe Title	Dear Mr. Doe
Mayor	The Honorable John Doe	Dear Mr. Mayor
Judge	The Honorable John Doe Judge of the _____ Court of _____	Dear Judge Doe
Clerk of the Court	John Doe, Esquire Clerk of the _____ Court of _____	Dear Mr. Doe

Foreign Service Officials

Ambassador	The Honorable John Doe United States Ambassador to _____	Dear Mr. Ambassador
Minister	The Honorable John Doe United States Minister to _____	Dear Mr. Minister
Charge d'affaires	John Doe, Esquire U.S. Charge d'affaires	Dear Mr. Doe
Consul General	John Doe, Esquire U.S. Consul General	Dear Mr. Doe

Foreign Diplomats and Officials

Ambassador	His Excellency, John Doe Ambassador of _____	Excellency, or Dear Mr. Ambassador
Prime Minister	His Excellency, John Doe Prime Minister of _____	Excellency, or Dear Mr. Prime Minister
British or Canadian Prime Minister	The Right Honorable John Doe Prime Minister	Dear Mr. Prime Minister
President of a Republic	His Excellency, John Doe President of _____	Excellency, or Dear Mr. President
Premier	His Excellency, John Doe Premier of _____	Excellency, or Dear Mr. Premier
Charge d'affaires	Mr. John Doe Charge d'affaires of _____	Dear Mr. Doe

United States Military

Officers	General John Doe, U.S.A.	Dear General Doe
Other personnel	Mr. John Doe, U.S.A.	Dear Mr. Doe
MILITARY ABBREVIATIONS:	Army	U.S.A.
	Air Force	U.S.A.F.
	Marine	U.S.M.C.
	Navy	U.S.N.
	Coast Guard	U.S.C.G.

Church Officials

Catholic

Pope	His Holiness Pope _____	Your Holiness
Cardinal	His Eminence, John Doe, D.D. Archbishop	Your Excellency, or
	_____	Dear Archbishop Doe
Bishop	The Most Reverend John Doe	Your Excellency, or Dear Bishop Doe
Abbot	The Right Reverend John Doe	Dear Father Doe, or Dear Father Abbot
Canon	The Reverend John Doe	Dear Canon Doe
Monsignor	The Right Reverend Msgr. John Doe	Right Reverend and Dear Monsignor Doe
Sister Superior	The Reverend Sister Superior	Dear Sister Superior

Protestant

Archbishop (Anglican)	To His Grace The Lord Archbishop of _____	Your Grace, or My Dear Archbishop
Methodist Bishop	The Reverend John Doe	Reverend Sir
Episcopal Bishop	The Right Reverend the Bishop of _____	Dear Bishop Sir
Presiding Bishop of the Episcopal Church in America	The Most Reverend John Doe Presiding Bishop of the Protestant Episcopal Church in America	Most Reverend Sir
Episcopal Priest	The Reverend John Doe	Dear Mr. Doe, or Dear Father Doe
Protestant Minister	The Reverend John Doe	Dear Mr. Doe

Jewish

Rabbi	Rabbi John Doe	Dear Rabbi Doe

High Education Officials

President (with Ph.D.)	John Doe, Ph.D. President, _____ College, or Dr. John Doe President, _____	Dear Dr. Doe
(without Ph.D.)	John Doe, President _____ College	Dear President Doe
Dean	Dean John Doe, or Dr. John Doe, Dean	Dear Dean Doe
Teaching Personnel (substitute proper rank)	John Doe, Ph.D. Professor	Dear Dr. Doe, or Dear Professor Doe

British Nobility

Duke	The Duke of _____	Dear Duke
Duchess	The Duchess of _____	Dear Duchess
Duke's younger son	The Lord John Doe	Dear Lord John
Wife of Duke's younger son	The Lady John Doe	Dear Lady John
Duke's daughter	The Lady Jane Doe	Dear Lady Jane
Marquess	The Marquess of _____	Dear Lord _____
Marchioness	The Marchioness of _____	Dear Lady _____
Earl	The Earl of _____	Dear Lord _____
Earl's wife	The Countess of _____	Dear Lady _____
Viscount	The Viscount _____	Dear Lord _____
Viscountess	The Viscountess _____	Dear Lady _____
Baron	The Lord _____	Dear Lord _____
Baroness	The Lady _____	Dear Lady _____
Baronet	Sir John Doe, Bart	Dear Sir John
Knight	Sir John Doe	Dear Sir John

INDEX

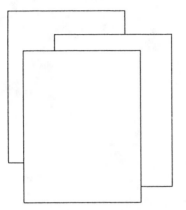

About the Author

Ted Nicholas is a multifaceted business personality. In addition to being a well-known author and respected speaker, Mr. Nicholas remains an active participant in his own entrepreneurial ventures. Without capital, he started his first business at age 21. Since then, he has started 22 companies of his own.

Mr. Nicholas has written 13 books on business and finance since his writing career began in 1972. The best known is *How To Form Your Own Corporation Without a Lawyer for under $75*. His previous business enterprises include Peterson's House of Fudge, a candy and ice cream manufacturing business conducted through 30 retail stores, as well as other businesses in franchising, real estate, machinery and food.

When the author was only 29, he was selected by a group of business leaders as one of the most outstanding businessmen in the nation and was invited to the White House to meet the President.

Although Mr. Nicholas has founded many successful enterprises, he also has experienced two major setbacks and many minor ones. He considers business setbacks necessary to success and the only true way to learn anything in life, a lesson that goes all the way back to childhood. That's why he teaches other entrepreneurs how to "fail forward."

Mr. Nicholas has appeared on numerous television and radio shows and conducts business seminars in Florida and Switzerland. Presently, he owns and operates four corporations of his own and acts as marketing consultant and copywriter to small as well as large businesses.

If you have any questions, thoughts or comments, Mr. Nicholas loves to hear from his readers! You are welcome to call, write or fax him at the following address:

Nicholas Direct, Inc.
19918 Gulf Boulevard, #7
Indian Shores, FL 34635
Phone: 813-596-4966
Fax: 813-596-6900

Keep Costs Down and Save Valuable Time & Effort–

Forms, Letters & Agreements Now Available on Computer Diskettes

Order Within 30 Days to Receive this Special Price!

 Now you can receive this complete collection of ***The Complete Guide to Business Agreements*** on diskette for just $29.95.

Think of the time and money you'll be able to save with these forms available to you at the press of a button! With our diskettes, you can use your word processing software to maximum advantage.

Designed to work with either the book in hand, or independent.

Diskettes are protected by warranty.

Diskette Only— Price: $~~69.95~~ $29.95

IBM and Compatibles:
5 1/4"   **Catalog #5615-56**
3 1/2"   **Catalog #5615-55**

 Normally sold separately for $69.95, now you can receive this complete collection of ***The Complete Book of Corporate Forms*** on diskette for just $29.95. Just think of the time and money you'll be able to save with these forms available to you at the press of a button! With our diskettes, you can use your word processing software to maximum advantage. Plus, forms are easily tailored to your specific situation:

• mix and match clauses
• generate multiple forms in succession
• alter layout to suit your style
• add or delete words or phrases

Designed to work with the book in hand!

Diskettes are protected by warranty.

Diskette Only— Price: $~~69.95~~ $29.95

IBM and Compatibles:
5 1/4"   **Catalog #5615-10**
3 1/2"   **Catalog #5615-11**

 Normally sold separately for $69.95, now you can receive this complete collection of ***The Executive's Business Letter Book*** on diskette for just $29.95. Just think of the time and money you'll be able to save with these letters available to you at the press of a button! With our diskettes, you can use your word processing software to maximum advantage. Plus, letters are easily tailored to your specific situation:

• mix and match clauses
• generate multiple forms in succession
• alter layout to suit your style
• add or delete words or phrases

Designed to work with the book in hand!

Diskettes are protected by warranty.

Diskette Only— Price: $~~69.95~~ $29.95

IBM and Compatibles:
5 1/4"   **Catalog #5615-19**
3 1/2"   **Catalog #5615-20**

Macintosh
3 1/2"   **Catalog #5615-21**

Send this coupon within 30 days of sales receipt and you'll receive the special $29.95 price!

☐ Send me the computer diskette for *The Complete Guide to Business Agreements*
IBM and Compatibles   ☐ 5 1/4"   ☐ 3 1/2"

☐ Send me the computer diskette for *The Complete Book of Corporate Forms*
IBM and Compatibles   ☐ 5 1/4"   ☐ 3 1/2"

☐ Send me the computer diskette for *The Executive's Business Letter Book*
IBM and Compatibles   ☐ 5 1/4"   ☐ 3 1/2"   ☐ Macintosh 3 1/2"

☐ Check enclosed payable to Enterprise • Dearborn

☐ Charge my   ☐ MasterCard   ☐ Visa

Account #_____ Exp. Date_____

Signature_____
(all charge orders must be signed)

Name_____

Firm_____

Address_____

City_____ State_____ Zip_____

Daytime Phone (_____)_____

MAIL TO: **Enterprise • Dearborn**
520 North Dearborn Street
Chicago, IL 60610-4354
Phone Orders: 1-800-854-7466

E10138